BUSES

YEARBOOK 2013

Edited by STEWART J. BROWN

KEY PUBLISHING

CONTENTS

© Key Publishing Ltd 2012

Published by Key Publishing Ltd.
www.keypublishing.com

Printed in England by
Berforts Information
Press Ltd, Southfield Road,
Eynsham, Oxford, OX29 4JB

First Published 2012

ISBN: 978 0 946219 36 0

Mixed Sources
Product group from well-managed
forests and other controlled sources

Cert no. SW-COC-004238
www.fsc.org
©1996 Forest Stewardship Council

Front Cover: One horse
power versus 115bhp as
a horse meets a London
Transport RT-class AEC
Regent III as it waits in the
Kent village of Downe before
setting off on the return run
up to Bromley in May 1978.
Tony Wilson

Back Cover (upper):
Illustrating the now standard
low-key hybrid branding,
an Arriva Volvo B5LH with
Wrightbus Gemini body
crosses Waterloo Bridge
heading north on route 76 to
Tottenham Town Hall.
Richard Walter

Back Cover (lower):
Blackpool standardised on
Leyland Titans with fully-fronted
centre-entrance bodywork for
its double-deckers between
1936 and 1950. Typifying
the final development of this
flamboyant style, which was
unique to Blackpool, is this bus
seen in St. Annes in July 1952.
John Hillmer

Previous page: The front
cover shows a London bus
widely accepted as a classic,
the RT-type. Prototypes of the
new Wrightbus-built LT class
entered service in 2012. Will it
be a future classic?
Richard Walter

The watering-can of corporatism

Discussion on corporate liveries is one topic that can get many bus enthusiasts hot under the collar.
GAVIN BOOTH explores.
All photographs by the author

There is a wonderful old film of London buses being painted at Chiswick, probably in London General days. It shows the painter, a watering-can full of paint in his hand, walking along beside a bus pouring paint on to the lower panels. A trough underneath the bus catches the drips – presumably for re-use. It all seemed so simple – so much so that at first I wondered if it was an April Fool hoax – but that was the way they did it and it seemed to work.

Of course this technique would only work with a comparatively straightforward livery, and with London buses currently reverting to a bland all-over red, maybe Alexander Dennis and Wrights could save money by investing in watering-cans rather than the sophisticated paint spray equipment they use. But then again ...

The red London buses hark back to the days when buses wore liveries that were simple to apply, as their application usually followed the lines of the bus, using raised mouldings to define where the colours should go. The convention was usually a predominant strong colour – red, green, blue – with a lighter relief colour – cream, off-white or white. Company buses wore proud fleetnames in gold shaded letters, often partly underlined. Municipal buses carried crests, which sometimes were enough to identify them, though some felt the need to add the name of the town or city, particularly where they were operating in the

The way it was – the traditional livery on this 1950 Morecambe & Heysham Corporation AEC Regent III with RT-style Park Royal body follows the lines of the bus and proclaims loudly whose bus it is.
Gavin Booth collection

areas of adjacent municipalities, but sometimes just because they could.

And for many years that was the way it was: buses could be easily identified, it was all very predictable and maybe just a wee bit boring.

The poet Philip Larkin wrote that sex was invented in 1963, "Between the end of the Chatterley ban and the Beatles' first LP", both events I remember well, though for different reasons. I would argue that interesting bus liveries were also invented in the 1960s, though later in that decade. In fact at the time the first Passenger Transport Executives and the National Bus Company were being created, though if these significant changes hadn't happened, I suspect we might still have seen brighter new liveries, but it might have taken a bit longer.

These changes swept away many of the traditional – and, yes, much-loved – liveries and introduced us to a new approach and to terms like 'corporate image' that we had only really associated with high street giants, multi-national industries and, in transport terms, London Transport.

So in 1969/70 out went 20 traditional municipal liveries to be replaced by five new PTE liveries – though when I say "new" ...

Out went eight blue liveries, plus five red/ maroon, five green and two yellow ones, and in came two blue, one orange, one green and one yellow. Thousands of hours of management time must have gone into merging very individual municipal undertakings into the government's exciting new PTEs, and we can only guess at the disproportionate number of hours spent in agreeing liveries, names and logos.

Though perhaps not at the new Tyneside and West Midlands PTEs, where there was little surprise

The orange livery adopted by the Selnec PTE looked good on rear-engined buses like this Park Royal-bodied Daimler Fleetline, seen after the PTE had become Greater Manchester Transport.

It was probably inevitable that the Tyneside PTE would adopt a livery largely based on Newcastle Corporation's colours, and this 1986 Alexander-bodied Leyland Olympian proclaims "I'm a new PTE Bus".

when something similar to the livery of the dominant municipality was adopted. Tyneside PTE had just two constituents – the physically separate Newcastle and South Shields undertakings – so the Newcastle yellow/cream was an obvious shoo-in. In the West Midlands, three of the fleets merged into the new PTE had blue buses (of widely differing hues) so poor green Wolverhampton lost out to blue Walsall and West Bromwich, which in turn lost out to a standard livery that turned out to be a slightly lighter variation of the Birmingham blue/cream.

Merseyside was initially a PTE of two halves, separated by the Mersey, with the green Liverpool area and the blue/primrose (blue for Birkenhead, primrose for Wallasey) Wirral livery; after a few

NBC poppy red, with only a white relief band – a Northern General Willowbrook-bodied Bristol VRT.

The first style of corporate Stagecoach livery used blue, red and orange stripes on a white background, as seen on a variety of vehicle types at the group's Fife Scottish company.

Badgerline, one of the constituents of FirstBus, used an amusing badger logo, here on an MCW Metrobus in Bristol.

years a new Verona green/cream was adopted.

Corporatism was very much in the air, so a couple of years after the Tilling and BET bus empires were merged into the new National Bus Company it was decided to sweep away a whole raft of familiar colours in favour of the rather unimaginative NBC standard schemes. The Tilling companies had long presented a more unified front with most buses in red or green, but BET companies had enjoyed a measure of individuality.

The new NBC colours were poppy red or leaf green, usually – but sadly not always – relieved by

a white band. A dark blue was initially introduced, but quickly dropped. Coaches became all-over white and dual-purpose vehicles were red or green with greater areas of white, arguably the most effective look.

The orangey-hued red was probably the more successful of the NBC colours, as the green seemed to fade more quickly. A new 'double-N' logo was devised with fleetnames in a corporate style and there was a detailed corporate identity manual – of course – to ensure that no managers stepped out of line. They did, of course. Little tweaks at first and then as the break-up of NBC loomed in the 1980s managers who had resented the centrally-imposed restrictions started to assert their individuality. As NBC companies were sold off new liveries emerged. Some were safe and sensible, while others reflected the pent-up frustration that many managers felt, and

Left: **In the days before the 'Barbie' livery became First's standard, the companies that had been taken over by Grampian wore this livery application in suitable colours with local fleetnames beside the 'flying F' logo, as on this Midland Bluebird MCW Metrobus with Alexander RL body.**

Although First's 'Barbie' livery was initially for low-floor buses with standard interiors, it soon spread to other types. This is a former Southampton City Transport Leyland Olympian/East Lancs.

Many felt that Arriva improved its aquamarine livery with the adoption of a darker blue skirt and blue upper deck front. This is an Alexander Dennis Enviro400 in Newcastle.

challenged the convention that bus liveries should follow the lines of the bus.

And as well as cocking a snook at NBC blandness there was another good reason to ensure that your buses stood out: deregulation. Not only had many former NBC managers committed their life savings and their houses to buy their companies, they faced the prospect of competition as the bus market was opened up to all comers. No longer did they have the safety net of route licensing monopolies, as competitors emerged to challenge their most profitable services. These newcomers often used brightly-painted second-hand buses so the incumbents had to protect their territories with eye-catching buses, including shoals of minibuses, seen as a low-cost way to safeguard the business and develop new routes. These were often in bright colours with splendidly silly names that caught the public's imagination. The Hoppas, Skippas and – probably – Jumpas had been born.

Then of course a new type of corporatism crept in as bus managers – or more likely their banks – realised that there was less and less money in the kitty to invest and build their businesses, so the larger and more financially secure companies stepped in, which led to the industry structure we have today, with the three mega-groups – Arriva,

First and Stagecoach – accounting for a substantial proportion of all bus journeys in Britain. They all ploughed the corporate identity furrow, returning us to the NBC days when company buses in virtually every town and city in England and Wales were either red or green – except that this now spread to Scotland too.

Stagecoach recognised the advantages of corporate colours from an early stage, when new buses for its growing empire were decked out in white with red, orange and blue Starsky & Hutch-type stripes; maybe it wasn't the most subtle image, but it was striking and as the company grew it made the transfer of buses between companies a fairly straightforward exercise and an argument was put forward that this would also reassure investors in the City that here was a major force in business. In 2000 the livery was freshened up using similar colours but applied in a gentler and subtler way.

First's main components – Grampian and Badgerline – had each started along the corporate road, Grampian with liveries applied in a standard style but using familiar colours, and Badgerline with the addition of badgers on the sides of its buses. These were swept away when the First identity was adopted and the 'Barbie' scheme was revealed – using a pale grey

Go North East's 'Whey Aye Five O' livery design – bright, eye-catching and a great pun.

London United adopted an attractive variant of London red with a grey skirt and roof, as worn by this Alexander Dennis ALX400 in Surbiton, after the London United identity had given way to the Transdev name.

with blue and magenta. So cities like Glasgow, Leeds and Sheffield that had distinctly-coloured municipal and even PTE buses were treated to large fleets of buses in colours that locals found it difficult to identify with. The situation was exacerbated by the adoption of what became known as 'Barbie 2', using the same colours but using vinyls where the colours deliberately faded to create the impression that, well, the colours had actually faded. Barbie 2, intended for older non-accessible buses, was quietly shelved and few tears were shed.

When Arriva was formed from the Cowie empire, it adopted a not unattractive aquamarine blue relieved with Cotswold Stone, but in recent years the livery has been tweaked, and arguably improved, with the inclusion of darker blue skirts and aquamarine fronts.

It was not long before local managers were wanting to adapt these corporate liveries and some attractive (and some pretty ghastly) variations emerged. The use of vinyl spread – literally; it was not only applied to the body sides but sometimes over windows as well, which may well have looked good in the designer's sketch, but took no account of the fact that paying passengers might actually want to see clearly out of the windows.

There are now remarkably few fleets in Britain where every bus is in the standard livery. Everyone, it seems, has recognised the value of buses as moving billboards and route branding has become king. For most operators, of course, a few main routes are branded and the rest of the fleet wears a generic livery. Others have followed the branding route almost to its ultimate terminus, with the majority of routes branded, and often very little to identify the operator. Trent Barton and Go North East lead the way with branding, and cities like Derby, Newcastle and Nottingham are awash with brightly-coloured buses carrying brandnames that are often references to local people or places. My favourite name is the wonderful pun worn by Go North East's 50 route linking Durham and South Shields, 'Whey Aye Five O', playing on the Geordie accent and the Hawaiian TV cop series. This is just one of over 40 brand identities used by Go North East, while Trent Barton has a similar number, with only a handful of routes identified by old-hat route numbers and a generic livery.

Bus enthusiasts tend to grumble about corporate liveries – but also, I suspect, about companies that brand virtually every route. Although they may moan about Go North East's multi-coloured fleet, they probably approve of Go North East's parent company, the Go-Ahead Group, which has followed a very non-corporate line, with just a tag-line telling people that their subsidiaries are part of the group. No one-colour-fits-all livery for this group, and some attractive company liveries like Oxford Bus, Southern Vectis and Wilts & Dorset.

Meanwhile London's buses have been moving away from what could strictly be called a 'livery' (defined in my dictionary as "the distinctive colours and decoration used to identify the buses, aircraft, etc operated by a particular company") to a single colour, red of course.

For a while after London routes first went out to tender in the 1980s operators were allowed to run buses in their own liveries – there were orange buses, blue/cream buses, yellow buses, brown/red/white buses, green/grey/orange buses. After privatisation more red was in evidence, but each operator added its own variations – yellow stripes for First, orange/blue rear swirls for Stagecoach, a cow's horn for Arriva and light grey tops for London United, for instance, but as Transport for London has exercised a tighter grip on its bus services, this has given way to a – let's face it – bland all-over red.

Finally some confessions. I am quite partial to

Above: **On a bright day the Edinburgh/Lothian madder and white could look good, but it lost its bloom very quickly and could look very dark. A 1991 Lothian Leyland Olympian/Alexander RH type in traditional colours.**

Right: **In 2010 Lothian adopted a new livery style using a colour similar to its traditional madder and applied in a contemporary way. This 2011 Volvo B9TL/Wright Gemini demonstrates the attractive result.**

Ray Stenning's designs for Best Impressions, and think Ray has done more than anyone to show how good 21st century liveries can be. I was a great fan of his London Country livery of the 1990s, and love the work he is doing for operators like Brighton & Hove, Reading Buses and Trent Barton. I know many bus companies take the view that they can manage perfectly well without the services (and cost) of a professional designer, but so often the results can look pretty shoddy.

Also – I was never very keen on the Edinburgh/Lothian madder and white livery. People think that I must surely have liked it, given my love of all things connected with that fleet. But no – it always seemed to go dull and brown very quickly, so I was a fan of the Lothian Buses harlequin livery when it was introduced on low-floor buses, and although Lothian has now reverted to something like its original madder colour, it is applied in an imaginative way and actually looks pretty good. Modern buses need modern liveries as many operators demonstrate

when they apply a heritage livery to a modern bus; somehow it never looks right.

Publications like *Buses Yearbook* are a long time in the preparation, and as I write this early in 2012 First has just unveiled its new corporate livery, giving more prominence to local names. So far I have only seen photos, so reserve my judgement, but by the time you read this there will be hundreds of buses in the new colours and the livery may already be old hat. But I do welcome the local aspect of the livery, something the big groups seemed to lose sight of in the early years of this century. Buses are an important part of the local scene and passengers don't always respond well to anonymous buses in liveries that represent, in the words of a former colleague, "the dead hand of the uninvolved". So let's see more of the branding that some fleets do so well, and let's see more tweaking of standard liveries to reflect local pride.

And let's say goodbye to the watering-can of corporatism.

Municipal
medley

A selection of municipal buses in the north-west of England captured by the camera of **JOHN HILLMER** in the early 1950s.

Captions by JOHN ROBINSON

Below: **Ashton-under-Lyne Corporation Passenger Transport Department (that's what it says on the waistband) took delivery of ten all-Leyland Titan PD2/3s in 1950. One is seen in Stockport in July 1952, wearing the then current livery of red, white and blue which gave way to a simpler peacock blue and cream in November 1954. Four of the Titans survived long enough to be acquired by the Selnec PTE in 1969, although none survived long enough to receive Selnec livery.**

Above: **For some years Lytham St. Annes standardised on Leyland buses with the manufacturer's Gearless torque converter transmission. Like neighbouring Blackpool it also favoured fully-fronted bodywork on its Leyland Titans for a time in the 1930s, and the result was vehicles like this all-Leyland Titan TD5c, one of four new in 1937. As can be seen in this view in St. Annes the design was far less flamboyant than Blackpool's with little more than a full-width cab being fitted to the standard Leyland body.**

Left: **Blackpool standardised on Leyland Titans with fully-fronted centre-entrance bodywork for its double-deckers between 1936 and 1950. The prototype streamlined body was constructed by English Electric on a TD4 chassis but all subsequent bodies were built in Blackpool by Burlingham. Typifying the final development of this flamboyant style, which was unique to Blackpool, is this bus seen in St. Annes in July 1952, from the last batch of 100 which was placed in service in 1949 and 1950. Based on PD2/5 chassis, these buses survived until the late 1960s.**

13

Left: **Between 1948 and 1951 Chester purchased ten Foden PVD6s, eight bodied by Massey and two by Davies. The latter bodywork proved unsatisfactory and these two were withdrawn after only seven years service. A 1949 Massey-bodied bus stands in St. Werburgh Street in July 1952 outside the city's fine cathedral. A Crosville Bristol L/ECW peers out from behind.**

Right: **The wonderfully-titled Stalybridge, Hyde, Mossley and Dukinfield Transport and Electricity Board (SHMD) was predominantly a Daimler fleet with Northern Counties bodying virtually all vehicles from 1926 onwards. A notable exception was a batch of ten Daimler CVD6s new in 1949 which were bodied by East Lancs, the only order received by the Blackburn bodybuilder from SHMD. This is an unusually deserted Lower Mosley Street bus station, Manchester, with the bus operating service 6 to Glossop which ran via Ashton and Stalybridge, jointly with Ashton, Manchester and North Western.**

Left: **Morecambe & Heysham was a major customer of AEC, with Regals and Regents being the only types purchased from 1932 until some Leyland Titans were delivered in 1960. This bus passing Central Pier on Morecambe's promenade on the route to Heysham Village on 7 June 1953, was one of twelve AEC Regent IIIs with Park Royal bodywork new in 1949. The rosette on the radiator appears to be a patriotic decoration for the coronation five days earlier. It was later one of several similar buses converted by the Corporation to open top, finally being withdrawn in 1979 when it was sold to a preservationist in Ireland. The operator had merged with Lancaster City Transport in April 1974 to form Lancaster City Council Transport Department which introduced a new livery of Trafalgar blue and white which this bus eventually received.**

Right: **Standing in Parker Street bus station (later re-named Piccadilly bus station), also in June 1953, this Manchester bus was one of 50 Metro-Cammell-bodied Daimler CVG6Ks (the K indicating axles supplied by Kirkstall Forge in Leeds instead of the more usual Daimler axle) new in 1950/51. Posters on two of the upper deck windows commemorate the coronation. Withdrawals commenced in 1968 but many of the batch survived to be transferred to the Selnec PTE in November 1969. All were gone by 1970.**

St. Helens was a major user of trolleybuses in Lancashire, operating a system from 1927 to final closure on 30 June 1958. This vehicle seen in Blackbrook in July 1952 on the Haydock service (operated jointly with South Lancashire Transport) was the last of a batch of ten Sunbeam MF2s with bodywork built by Massey in neighbouring Wigan. The chassis of these vehicles were intended for Johannesburg but because of the war were allocated to St. Helens, entering service in 1942. As the chassis were 8ft wide and the maximum permitted width in Britain at the time was 7ft 6ins, dispensation had to be obtained to operate these vehicles which, in turn, demonstrated that operation at this width was perfectly practical, paving the way for the adoption of an 8ft limit in Britain in 1950. These were the only 8ft wide trolleybuses ever fitted with lowbridge bodies which accounts for their very squat appearance.

When Duple ceased to be Dominant

The 1980 deregulation of the UK's express coach services had a serious impact on Duple's output. The long running Duple Dominant coach was replaced by a new range of bodies from 1982; **DAVID JUKES** examines these and subsequent production until the company's 1989 demise.

All photographs by the author

Duple was the dominant force in British coachbuilding until 1969 when its main competitor, Plaxton of Scarborough, caught up with and then overtook Duple's annual output. The metal-framed Dominant, which was introduced in 1972, helped Duple regain some of the lost ground but only to the extent of raising its annual sales to around 70% of Plaxton's, where they were to remain throughout the 1970s.

Operator uncertainty caused by the deregulation of express coach services in 1980 adversely affected both coachbuilders. But it was Blackpool-based Duple that suffered most as it bodied a greater proportion of lightweight Bedford and Ford coach chassis than its east coast rival, a market that all but dried up overnight as operators able to afford new vehicles switched to heavyweight alternatives.

The 1980s began with Duple producing the Dominant coach in four forms: the original I of 1972, the 1976 restyled II and, from 1980, the trapezoid-windowed III and the raised waistline IV. These were supplemented by the Dominant bus which was introduced in 1975 and had little in common with its namesake coaches. To these was added the Goldliner range in time for the 1982 season; this was, in essence, a high-floor Dominant with the II, III and IV side window styles.

In 1980 production of just over 800 home market bodies was followed by the delivery of around 500 the following year and 449 in 1982. September 1982

This preserved ex-Southdown Laser-bodied Leyland Tiger has been restored to its original National Holidays livery and is seen on Brighton's Madeira Drive during the Brighton & Hove 75th Anniversary event in June 2010. It was new in the spring of 1984.

saw Duple announce a new range of coach bodies, the normal height Laser and high-floor Caribbean, with which Duple intended to regain some of its lost market. The Dominant III and IV plus (unofficially) the Goldliner remained in production during 1983 alongside the Dominant bus, which was ultimately to remain available until 1988.

The Laser and Caribbean were launched at the 1982 Motor Show. The former introduced a new concept of improved aerodynamic efficiency; its most noticeable feature being a rounded front end incorporating a noticeably raked windscreen. The curvaceous Laser also incorporated radiused window frames and, while looking most individualistic when compared to its contemporaries from other coachbuilders, bore an element of family resemblance

to the Dominant.

In contrast, the Caribbean was much squarer than the Laser with a deeper less raked windscreen and more upright sides containing window frames which were less radiused than its lower height sister but were still gasket mounted. The Caribbean's profile recalled many of the more angular designs emanating from the mainstream European coachbuilders during the late 1970s.

The Laser and Caribbean were fitted with identical lower front panels, which were distinguished by a pair of rectangular headlights, and vertical brightwork embellishments located immediately behind the passenger door and driver's side window – that on the Laser hanging lower owing to its lower build height. In essence, that was the sum of family

Left: The Calypso looked like a low-built Caribbean. This one was new to Cook's Coaches of Westcliff in late 1984, carrying cherished registration number WWC 820 from new. It is seen at Clarence Pier coach park, Portsmouth, in 1990. Its continental door has required the fitting of a shallow window amidships; a conventional emergency exit is also fitted at the offside rear.

This Southend Transport 1984 Caribbean-bodied Leyland Tiger forms part of the Ensignbus heritage fleet. It is seen restored to original livery at the 2010 Cobham Bus Museum Spring Gathering.

The restyling which created the Laser 2 is illustrated by this 1986 Bedford YNV operated by Dudley Coachways and seen in York in 1988. The bonded glazing, single-piece windscreen and new style grille are clearly visible.

A 1984 Leyland Tiger with Laser 2 body in the Wilts & Dorset fleet departs Heathrow central bus station in August 1989. The coach is fitted with two piece entrance doors for express coach service operation. The grille surround is painted in fleet livery – an option offered by Duple.

resemblance between the two models.

Duple introduced new techniques to produce the Laser and Caribbean; floor frames, sideframes, ends and roofs were jig-built and married together to create a complete self-supporting body frame. Only then was the chassis added, after mounting brackets and heater connections had been fitted elsewhere in the factory.

A self-supporting body structure can render a conventional chassis unnecessary; the Caribbean was initially intended as an integral using a Neoplan underframe. A single Mercedes-Benz-powered example was built and registered by Duple but it was soon superseded in the project stakes by a partnership with Bova, from which the Duple Calypso resulted. The Calypso used Bova's EL26 underframe beneath a Caribbean-style body but constructed to the lower Laser height. Both integral types introduced bonded glazing to this generation of Duple bodywork; the Calypso also carried a revised front end incorporating single rectangular headlights with as a result a wider grille. The Calypso made its debut at the 1983 British Coach Rally alongside the Caribbean integral. Fifty Calypsos were ultimately constructed for sole distribution by the Moseley dealership, while the integral Caribbean remained unique.

June 1983 saw Duple sold to the Hestair Group, owners of Dennis. Duple was soon renamed Hestair Duple Ltd and its production facilities reorganised to permit greater efficiencies from a smaller workforce. A new paint shop was commissioned as part of this work.

Hestair's ownership was initially marked by styling changes to the Laser and Caribbean; the former being made available with a single-piece windscreen and both having the Calypso-style lower front panels as an option. The Caribbean integral was also re-engined with a Cummins L10 in preparation for a third Duple integral coach project; this time to be developed in-house with engineering input from Hestair Dennis.

But 1983's production of just 84 Laser and 68 Caribbean bodies did little to encourage the company's new owners, particularly as both types were outnumbered by the final year's output of the Dominant coach. The following year saw Duple's total production drop further, although it was fortunately boosted by the aforementioned Calypsos. More worryingly, Duple had been overtaken by Van Hool in sales to independent operators.

The run up to 1984's Motor Show saw Duple announce styling alterations to its coach bodies. The

Laser 2 and Caribbean II (the mix of Arabic and Roman numerals was deliberate) were the results of an exercise by John Worker Design which introduced bonded glazing as standard and a redesigned lower front panel with single headlights for both types, a standard single-piece windscreen for the Laser 2 and optional single-piece windscreen for the Caribbean II.

Examples of both were displayed on Duple's stand at the Motor Show but these were eclipsed by a new stable mate, the Integral 425, which Duple successfully kept under wraps until its unveiling at Birmingham. The all-new 425, the result of Duple's third integral coach project, was developed for maximum economy using the fuel efficient Cummins LT10 engine and specially designed by John Worker Design to have a very low drag coefficient. Its distinctive front, gently curved and topped by a sharply raked tinted glass dome, allied with bonded side glazing and steel panels, not to mention a glass fibre roof, resulted in a smooth profile and a drag coefficient of 0.425 – hence the model's name – which was claimed at the time by Duple to be the lowest for any coach.

Use of chassisless construction and lightweight materials reduced the Integral 425's unladen weight to a respectable 10.5 tonnes, further assisting its operational economy. Duple was able to provide a massive 14 cubic metres of luggage capacity and could fit 63 seats into the passenger saloon using a new seating unit that incorporated a shorter squab and more upright back, although most operators of the type preferred to specify less than maximum capacity thereby increasing passenger legroom and comfort.

Volume production of the Integral 425 started in earnest towards the end of 1985 but its introduction, together with those of the Laser 2 and Caribbean II, did not prevent a further slide in Duple's home market sales total for that year. Duple clearly considered its share in the Laser and Caribbean-type market sectors to be inadequate and sought instead to offer something new. It introduced two new coach bodies in late 1985 to replace both of these despite their introduction just three years previously and a major restyling for the 1985 season.

The resulting 320 and 340 bodies were low-floor and high-floor versions of a common theme – the model names representing their overall heights measured in centimetres. Both owed a little to the Caribbean in shape and the Integral 425 in construction technology. Duple sought to maximise

The Integral 425 was a distinctive coach. This example was new in 1986 to Whittle of Kidderminster and is seen in Chichester 21 years later in the ownership of Arun Coaches of Horsham.

Portsmouth Coaches operated this 320-bodied DAF SB2305 which had been new in 1988 to Holt of Reedness. This is a 2002 view at the Worthing Bus Running Day and Rally.

Warrens of Ticehurst operated this 1989 320-bodied Scania K92CRB, seen in a Bath coach park in 1992. The Scania/320 body combination was unusual.

A 1987 Kelvin Scottish Leyland Tiger illustrates the high-floor 340 body as it turns into Pond Street bus station, Sheffield, in the summer of 1989. The body is fitted with a two-piece windscreen and a rear-mounted continental door/emergency exit. The fitting of an identical windscreen and lower front panel to the 320 and 340 required the latter model's roof to slope down above the windscreen.

the use of parts common to the 320 and 340 which, in turn, led to the most distinctive difference between the two; the 320 having a flat roof while the 340's roof sloped downwards at the front to meet the windscreen. The windscreen was common to both models and surmounted a new lower front panel of smoother profile than that fitted to the preceding Laser and Caribbean models. The roof at the rear of the 320 and 340 was raised to incorporate an advanced heating and ventilation system that enabled Duple to do away with conventional opening rooflights. Bonded glazing and side panels were also fitted to both types as standard.

The Integral 425 did not escape attention either. It was made available with the DAF 11.6-litre DKSB engine as an option to the 10-litre Cummins unit initially fitted, and received a number of structural modifications.

Duple's 1986 order book held firm but dropped to 176 coach and seven bus bodies the following year. 1988 saw the figures increase to 233 and 15 respectively – approximately a third of the coach bodies being built on the newly introduced Dennis Javelin chassis, seen by many within the industry as a worthy successor to the short-lived Bedford Venturer.

The Dominant bus body was finally phased out during 1988. Its replacement, the 300, was based on the structure used beneath the 320 and 340 coach bodies; its designation once again recognising its overall height in centimetres. The 300 was a relatively plain design but utilised the 320/340 front grille, thereby outwardly retaining the family relationship.

Another Duple bus body appeared in 1988. This was a stainless-steel-framed, aluminium-panelled structure specifically produced for mounting on the newly introduced Dennis Dart rear-engined midi-bus chassis. The new body, later to be christened the Dartline, was based on the 300-series but incorporated an unusual curved front profile; a convex curved windscreen surmounted a concave-curved plain lower front panel. Hestair initially intended the Dart chassis to be offered solely with the Duple body but subsequent events caused a change of plan.

The Hestair Group announced the sale of its vehicle engineering division to a management buy-out team in November 1988 – the new owners, Trinity Holdings, taking over in January 1989. A new future beckoned, but it was not to last.

The closure of Duple's operations was announced

First Eastern Counties operated this 1989 300-bodied Dennis Javelin, which was one of five supplied to the company while it was still privately-owned. It had 48 high-backed seats and is seen in Norwich in September 1997.

Great Yarmouth Transport purchased a trio of Duple-bodied Dennis Darts in 1990. One is seen in the town in July 1990 when three months old.

It looks like a Duple 320, but the badge on the front shows that this is in fact a Plaxton 321 – looking very smart at the 2007 Showbus rally.

in July 1989. Its spares and repair subsidiary, Duple Services Ltd, together with the manufacturing rights and jigs for the 300, 320, 340 and Integral 425 bodies were immediately sold to Plaxton. The Vicarage Lane factory remained in the Trinity Group's ownership and continued to produce bodies for the Dennis Dart until that October when the Carlyle Group acquired the Dartline's manufacturing rights, jigs and order books. Duple's four prototypes were followed by 58 Blackpool-built production examples before body manufacture moved to Birmingham.

But that was not quite the end. Plaxton built a single batch of coaches to the Duple 320 design, and marketed this as the Plaxton 321. Twenty-five were built in 1989/90 on Leyland Tiger chassis and were made available through the W S Yeates dealership in Loughborough. The 321 utilised interior fittings and external mouldings from Plaxton's Paramount range.

Plaxton also went on to build the Integral 425 in France at its Carrosserie Lorraine subsidiary during 1991. The announcement of the Plaxton 425's production, which featured new interior trim and other modifications to the original Duple model, was all too swiftly followed by news of the Carrosserie Lorraine plant's closure with just 12 of the type built. Plaxton intended to restart production at Scarborough but, like the 321, no more were to be built.

The Carlyle Bus Centre went into liquidation in late 1991 with its designs, manufacturing rights,

This Emsworth & District Duple-bodied Dart was new to London Buses in 1990. It reached Emsworth & District via Southern Vectis, which fitted its large destination box, answering a criticism that the original destination display behind the windscreen (as on the Great Yarmouth bus opposite) could be hard to read. It is seen in Havant in November 2010.

fixtures and fittings passing to Marshall of Cambridge. Production of the Dartline restarted in a small way at its new home during 1992 before the body was revamped as a Marshall product from 1993.

But that is not all. We turn the clock back to 1981 when Duple International formed a new company – Duple (Metsec) Ltd – to take over and continue the bus bodybuilding business of TI Metsec, which had long been engaged in the construction of bus bodies in completely knocked down (CKD) kit form for assembly overseas. Ownership of Duple (Metsec) was retained by Trinity Holdings after the sale and closure of Duple in 1989. It passed to the Mayflower Corporation with fellow Trinity constituent Dennis in 1998, but the formation of the joint Mayflower/Plaxton venture in 2000 (as TransBus International) led to its demise – the Duple (Metsec) doors closing the following year.

Examples of Duple's post-Dominant products have entered preservation or remain in service at the time of writing. A fine array of Integral 425s has been a regular feature of the most recent Showbus gatherings while Emsworth & District, this writer's local independent, regularly operates the 47th production Dartline built (ex-London Buses DT16) which is now into its 21st year of service. And there remain plenty of Duple (Metsec)-bodied Dennis Condors and Dragons in operation across the UK after their return from the Far East, arguably the most high profile of these being the Big Bus Company's fleet of London sightseeing open-toppers.

When Duple's Blackpool factory closed the associated Duple (Metsec) business continued as a builder of CKD kits for export markets. This Dennis Condor was supplied to the China Motor Bus Co in Hong Kong in 1989 but was later purchased by the Big Bus Company and converted to partial open-top for operation on London sightseeing tours.

When photographed in May 1989, this Northern Counties-bodied Dennis Dominator was one of the last still wearing the original Cleveland Transit livery. It is seen in Middlesbrough. The fleet number has an H prefix, applied to buses which could not pass beneath the railway bridge at Middlesbrough station.

Colourful Cleveland

MARK BAILEY takes a look at bus operations in Cleveland in the years following local bus service deregulation in 1986.

The county of Cleveland had a brief existence. It came into being on 1 April 1974 as a result of Local Government reorganisation and was formed from parts of the North Riding of Yorkshire and County Durham. The main centres of population were Middlesbrough, Stockton-on-Tees, Hartlepool, Billingham, Redcar and Guisborough. It was abolished on 1 April 1996, being superseded by four unitary authorities.

At the time of its formation the dominant bus operators were National Bus Company subsidiary United Automobile Services, Cleveland Transit (the successor to Teesside Municipal Transport) and

Hartlepool Borough Transport. In December 1987 United was privatised and later broken up into smaller companies - after several changes of ownership most would be reunited within the Arriva group. In the early 1990s both municipal operators were bought out by their employees, and in November 1994 and January 1995 they in turn sold out to the expanding Stagecoach empire.

This selection illustrates the varied and colourful scene during the latter years of Cleveland county's existence, as the consequences of local bus deregulation and privatisation unfolded, and before the liveries of the new major groups took hold.

Stockton's magnificent town hall, set in its wide High Street, forms the backdrop to this May 1989 view of a Northern Counties-bodied Leyland Fleetline. Middlesbrough Corporation had operated Daimler Fleetlines in large numbers since the early 1960s, and this was the very last one delivered to successor Cleveland Transit, entering service towards the end of 1983. It was also the last Fleetline to enter service anywhere.

Many fleets received an influx of minibuses in the mid to late 1980s, and Cleveland Transit was no exception. Four Northern Counties-bodied Dodge S56s were delivered in 1986; this example was pictured in May 1989 at Port Clarence departing on service 68 to the North Tees Hospital. Note the unusual single-piece door.

Among the last new vehicles for Cleveland Transit before its sale to the Stagecoach group were a dozen Plaxton Verde-bodied Volvo B10Bs delivered in 1994. Stagecoach retained the Cleveland Transit identity and livery for a time, and the only visible sign of the new order was the modified wording under the Transit fleetname, which now read 'Part of the Stagecoach Group'. One of the Verdes is seen in August 1995 in Middlesbrough bus station, departing for Hartlepool on service 10.

Seen in August 1993 on a Stockton local service is Cleveland Transit's solitary open-topper, a Northern Counties-bodied Leyland Titan PD3/4 new to Southdown. Route 58 to the Hardwick Estate had seen intense competition since deregulation, but on this day rival operators Robson and Delta were struggling to match the appeal of riding upstairs on an open-top bus.

Hartlepool Transport operated a dozen Dennis Falcons, the first six of which were delivered in 1983 and had Wadham Stringer dual-door bodywork. One is seen waiting in Victoria Road in May 1989 on cross-town service 7 to Old Hartlepool with 'Your Bus' lettering to stress the fleet's local ownership.

Between 1967 and 1975 Hartlepool Borough Transport bought 57 ECW dual-door Bristol RELL6Ls. One of the final batch turns into Middlegate bus station in Old Hartlepool in August 1993.

Left: **Tees & District operated several Leyland Lynx IIs, identifiable by a protruding grille designed to accommodate an intercooler. One is pictured in Stockton High Street in August 1993 on service 268. This route traversed Cleveland from Lingdale in the east through to Darlington, in County Durham, in the west.**

Below: **In February 1990 part of United's operations was split away to form Tees & District, and yellow was added to United's existing red and white livery. Illustrating this is an ECW-bodied Bristol VRTSL6G, seen in June 1991 in Sunderland's Park Lane bus station on the 230 service to Hartlepool.**

Above: **Deregulation in 1986 gave County Durham operator Trimdon Motor Services opportunities to expand into new territory. It introduced services in competition with Cleveland Transit and secured tendered work from Cleveland County Council, amassing a fleet of second-hand ECW-bodied Bristol LH6Ls. The operations grew to such a size that in April 1989 a separate company was created, Teesside Motor Services. Typifying the fleet is a former Bristol Omnibus LH, seen in Middlesbrough in May 1989 working service 11 from Coulby Newham.**

Right: **In the early 1990s 51 Optare Vecta-bodied MAN 11.190s were delivered to Teesside Motor Services and associated fleets. Seen in Stockton in August 1995 is a 1993 bus working on service 116 from Roseworth to Cunningham Drive, Thornaby. The Vectas were 42-seaters.**

Robson of Thornaby-on-Tees commenced operations on deregulation day in 1986 with a pair of Ford Transits, graduating to bigger vehicles as loadings increased. In May 1989 a 10-year-old ECW-bodied Bristol LHS6L which had been new to Northampton Transport is seen passing Stockton's street market on the Crooksbarn service.

For a short while this ECW coach-seated Leyland Olympian of United sported a distinctive red and blue livery. On a lovely Saturday at the end of May 1989 it is seen departing from Middlesbrough with what looks like a full load for Scarborough.

Delta, based in Stockton-on-Tees, standardised on the Bristol RE for local bus operations. Typical of the fleet was this ECW-bodied RESL6G which had been new in 1972 to United. It was pictured in Middlesbrough in May 1989 whilst working service 37 to Park End.

Above: **Wilson of Middlesbrough traded as Escort and operated local services to Nunthorpe and Marton. Pictured on route 102 in May 1989 is an Alexander-bodied Leyland Leopard PSU3/3R that had been new to Eastern Scottish.**

Below: **Following local bus deregulation, OK Travel expanded significantly in size and territory beyond its Bishop Auckland heartland, including securing some Cleveland County Council tendered work. Seen in Middlesbrough in August 1995 is a Plaxton-bodied Volvo B6 registered L405 GDC and lettered, coincidentally, for service 405. A few months earlier, in March, OK had sold out to the Go-Ahead Group.**

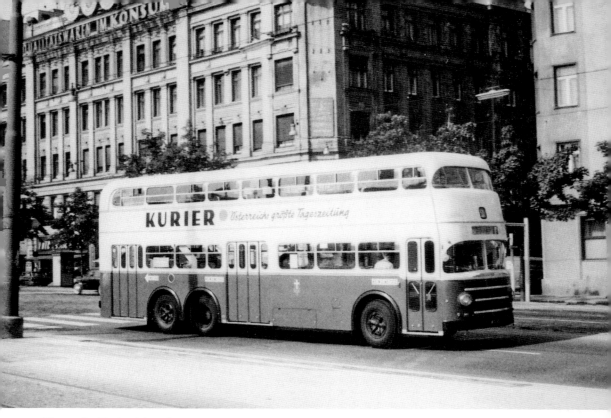

Vienna in 1963 with a three-door, three-axle double-decker built by Austrian manufacturer Gräf & Stift.

The fool and his folly

"So a fool returneth to his folly." Thus is it stated in Proverbs XXVI, v11. I refrain from quoting the first half of this text, lest it offend the sensibilities of my readers, but of course they (my readers, not their sensibilities) can readily search it out for themselves from the Holy Writ in their shelves as easily as they can pluck forth earlier editions of *Buses Yearbook*. As is my custom – though not in this volume giving way to interludes with long-lost sweethearts – I must return to issues with which I have dwelt hitherto in these pages, and, to whit, my profound affection for the three-axle double-decker.

Now save for giving notice that the first time I attacked this topic was as ago long as in *Buses Annual*

ROBERT E. JOWITT wallows in fond memories of earlier generations of Continental three-axle double-deckers, and the difficulties of catching their present-day successors.

1973, I do not propose to clutter these pages with the precise dates of my further venturing into the matter; most if not all of such of my perambulations in the field are in more recent years and my reader may spend a pleasant Sunday afternoon turning over the pages of the latest decade of *Buses Yearbooks* to encounter much enjoyment and useful instruction quite apart from anything offered by my own *opuscula*. Students of Latin will translate this term as 'small works', which interpretation, though correct, sounds to me rather like the efforts of minor jerry-builders, and anyway I think the Latin word is fine enough to merit an airing in publication.

Thus forthwith, excluding the London Transport LT upon which I lavished some praise last year but

Torino's striking three-axle double-deckers were built by Viberti and had a vertical Fiat engine located behind the front offside wheel. They had two staircases, as can be clearly seen. This is a 1966 view.

An ex-London trolleybus in Bilbao in 1969.

which the reader may well argue, given the subtitle of this article, that the LT is not Continental, and ignoring a Parisian open-top prototype, pre 1914, possibly a Brillie-Schneider, briefly studied by the French army, but probably never in passenger service, I must start upon this essay – or *opusculum* – by referring to my acquaintance with early picture postcards of Berlin. Berlin had a major persuasion to double-deckers, initially much like London's B-types, developing, in the dreadful inter-war-years of Weimar and worse, into huge vehicles, by Büssing, I suspect, double-deck, three-axle, a huge snout afore, intermingling in the streets with Storm-troopers and Hitlerjugend. It can be admitted that these buses were as typical of Berlin as were the open-platform Renaults of Paris or the red double-deckers of London.

If any survived the war I do not know, but Berlin continued with double-deckers thereafter, albeit two-axle and flat-fronted, now much beloved by model-makers and picture-postcard publishers.

I may say I have never visited Berlin, nor ever wanted to, for, despite travellers' tales of a vibrant lively city, I fear I might find 'bad vibes' rather than vibrancy. I found such to be the case in Hamburg, where I spent a day or two in 1963, and, in spite of the remnants of a once splendid tram system, with cars totally unlike your average German vehicles, I found the aura of the place depressing in the extreme.

I would not, in the context of this essay, make mention of Hamburg were it not that one of its suburbs, namely Harburg, relished a brief but glamorous flirtation, between 1953 and 1957, with five very handsome Henschell three-axle double-deck, double-stairs, double-entrance trolleybuses. Had someone in Harburg, Hamburg or Henschell been inspired by the light of a Bournemouth Corporation Sunbeam? But these beauties were transferred to Erfurt and cut down to fairly boring single-deckers, the last scrapped in 1965.

Except in Great Britain, or places in her sway such as Commonwealth and Colonies, and apart from the Harburg lark, three-axle double-deck trolleybuses were almost unknown, but British influence – even if politically we may wonder why – produced ten very London-type 60-seater vehicles in 1938 in Moscow, though as to where they were built I must profess ignorance. Given this date their existence and their following career – if any – must be regarded as almost akin to mythical. All subsequent Moscow trolleybuses, numbered in well over a thousand, were single deck, some articulated – even unto four axles – and thoroughly Russian... and then some!

The Great British three-axle double-deck trolleybus made nevertheless a major mark upon European soil – or, at least, Iberian soil – initially, so historians tell us, with, in the late 1940s, between 20 and 30 British-built BUTs new for Barcelona; and then the well-known sale of a large quantity of second-hand London trolleybuses, not long before the final demise of the world's greatest trolleybus system, to various spots in Spain.

The said Great British trolleybus, as the epitome or heart and soul of British trolleybus art, could be numbered with little hesitation by anyone who loves such issues as present on at least a dozen British systems. Its revival in Spain was a strange affair, with the Spaniards cutting the London trolleybuses about in diverse forms to suit their diverse rejuvenation. The tale has oft been told, and I myself have related passages, but here I must once again repeat, be it ever briefly, the transmogrification of two vehicles. I refer to the celebrated saga of Bilbao – where most ex-Londoners remained red and, serving the docks, not at all un-Londonish – with two suffering an extra 1½ windows spliced into the body and converted, with trolley gear ousted, to Leyland Worldmaster diesels, rendering them, at that date at least, surely among Europe's largest three-axle double-deck motor buses.

None the less, in those days there were other giants. In Vienna, in 1963, when tram-hunting in a paradise as divine as, and in some ways not unlike, the late Glasgow, I encountered one route given over

The great conversion: one of two ex-London trolleybuses in Bilbao with an extra one-and-a-half windows spliced in, and power supplied by a Leyland Worldmaster engine. This is a 1969 view.

to enormous three-axle double-deck buses, of some local manufacture though half a century later I recall not which, these installed, so I understood, to replace a tramline which had proved difficult, though I wondered if mammoth buses might not prove more difficult. I expect I rode upon them at the time, but equally, given now the lapse of time, I cannot remember. I was in Vienna for trams!

The same case applies to Torino, Italy, a couple of years later. Italy had long, on occasion, espoused double-deck practice, with, in Milano, formidable trams *plus* trailers in the primitive years, and, more recently, double-deck buses in Rome, albeit mere two-axles, with the back of the roof sloping down like an upturned wheel-barrow or the rump of an early Standard Vanguard. But Torino, in 1966, revealed a route, among many other entrancements, of magnificent three-axle double-deck buses! Were they tram replacements I had no means of discovering, my Italian being not up to my German, or in fact virtually non-existent, most inconvenient for arguing with shark restaurant proprietors, but they were, like the Viennese double-deckers and the Viennese trams, and unlike the usual boring two-tone green of the Torino trams, (or, come to that, the Milano trams and the Genova trolleybuses and for all I know most other trams and trolleybuses in Italy) in splendid red and cream. They appeared as of monstrous size similar to the Viennese, they may have been even larger, they may, if I can hazard a guess, have been Fiat or OM, but, unlike the uncompromising almost Hapsburg glower of their Vienna counterparts, the Torino examples rejoiced in a Gina Lollobrigida or Sophia Loren quality of curvaceous lines. Though memory once again fails me I suspect that, given my lack of Italian, I eschewed the hazard of attempting to travel on them.

It must be plain to the reader that the encounters described so far are of at least 40 years ago, and that thereafter, given the frailty of buses, or at very least the more exotic buses, and given also that my travels thereafter did not take me to places where such florid buses might be found, I fell to imagining or assuming

Great Eastern heroes returning to their native shores, some to operate for a while in Manchester as ordinary buses, and others to be hacked about and to a greater or lesser extent un-roofed to serve as London sight-seeing buses. Now despite my predilection for second-hand buses serving in other roles (such as mobile chip-shops or hippie caravans) I have never, for some strange reason, acquired any great affection for sight-seeing buses. I particularly dislike purpose-built buses of this ilk, considering that the proper way to explore any city is to travel on the common service bus, difficult by linguistic problems though this may prove. Give me the good old days of the Paris open-platforms, even the present day Clapham omnibus, not Paris Vision or Guide Friday or even the erstwhile Obsolete Fleet.

Setting such deviations aside (and we may note that neither Manchester, London, nor Hong Kong may be included in the reference to the Continent, viz Europe, which is the subject of these words) I made a return visit after my first visit thither, in 1962 when the last tram route was still functioning if not flourishing, to Luxembourg, in the early years of the present century. This proved entirely to my taste, revealing a thriving and intensive bus service which included many articulateds – and, on subsequent visits, an increasing number of three-part articulateds (or tri-partites, or, as they are locally, charmingly described *double-accordeon!*) and a quantity of lengthily superb three-axle single-deckers. To add to this, when I was admiring the great Pont Adolphe from a distance of some 200 yards or more, a three-axle *double-decker* sped over it. Later I saw this divine spectacle again – it was in the colours of Emile Weber, a large local and inter-urban bus and coach operator – parked in the Rue Heine, when I was on a bus from which, for now some forgotten reason, it was imperative that I did not alight. Then again I sighted it, up near the Park where I was photographically engaged, but, as if it knew I was after it, it turned away coyly into a side street before it was anywhere near me.

that these outlandish practices were soon giving way to more normal notions.

And then, nevertheless, a decade or so later, when it might have been reasonable to suppose, especially in what was largely deemed a decaying bus industry world-wide (hurrah for the private car), the idea of the three-axle double-decker was lost and gone forever (Oh, my darling Clementine!) there were signs of a resurgence...

Both in England and on the Continent, in the field of express coaches – not a field for which, I freely admit, I have much enthusiasm – there arose a revival, while out in the Far East, or Hong Kong and thereabouts, vast British-built three-axle double-deckers were taking to the streets. By chance observation of the former and chance study in bus magazines of the latter I chanced on this information, but I was not given to travelling by coach in Britain, and Hong Kong was far too far away to be of more than passing interest.

If we move onwards another decade we find the

Eventually, on my next visit, a year or so later, I

finally caught the beast sitting peacefully on the lay-over bay by the Rose Garden. This might have meant that it was soon to go across the road to the Rue Heine to load.... But equally it might not. At least I had the chance to shoot it, before moving on to whatever else I was supposed to be doing... and not catching a ride on it....

Before recounting third (or any other) encounters with this bus, or attempts to ride on it, I feel bound to indulge in some digression. The second digression is about other similar buses but the first is as follows: On my first sight of any three-axle buses in Luxembourg in the early 2000s I made the assumption that they were all utterly new and up-to-date. Well, they were all spotlessly clean and unblemished. I am not given, on the whole, to reading up-to-date transport journals – though a rare exception to this set me off in search of the four-axle articulateds in Stuttgart and St. Gallen – for I prefer to take the scene, in blissful ignorance though possibly to my detriment, as I find it, and perhaps to find out more about it afterwards. As is well known, I believe, it is not so much the buses themselves as the buses in their surroundings which charm me most. It therefore came to me as something of a shock, in the autumn of 2011, when purchasing a grandly expensive book on transport in the city of Luxembourg, to discover a photograph dating back to at least 1993 including a three-axle double-decker.

Weber's three-axle double-decker on layover by the Rose Garden in Luxembourg

Another Weber double-decker leaving Canach, just visible in the background, as it heads towards the company's depot on the edge of the village.

This example was actually with Demy Cars, who, probably, come close behind Weber in supplying transport to the Luxembourg area. I have never seen a Demy Cars double-decker in Luxembourg, I even could wonder if they passed theirs on to Weber. I have no means of knowing, not that it particularly worries me, but plainly the affair is far older than I had first imagined; these double-deckers could be close on 20 years old!

Passing on to my second digression, or from Luxembourg to St. Gallen, Switzerland, in pursuit of the MAN four-axle bus. Here, oh, rapture, apart from trolleybuses, was a regular flow or tide of three-axle double-deckers in Swiss Postal service. Swiss Post buses are famous and almost legendary in their habit – does it, I wonder, still prevail – in having special traffic signs bidding all on-coming traffic give way to them. I doubt any oncoming motorist would try to battle with one of these St. Gallen goliaths, for

they are as large as and largely similar – or almost identical! – to the Luxembourg variety, and as heavy-duty as Viennese or Torino heroes of antiquity.

I do not know what make or body they are, any more than I can answer such questions about Luxembourg (save only that in St. Gallen Neoplan is boasted largely on the front). I simply gazed at them in adoration, and it is to my infinite regret that, being closely bound up with pursuing the MAN and a home-made tripartite trolleybus I did not have the opportunity to adventure into a journey on them into, I must assume, that divinely rumply neat countryside which, once freed of ultimately hideous light industry – as I know from railway travel – surrounds St. Gallen. Subsequent studies of timetables have implied I might either have enjoyed rural rides or found myself in dismal outskirts. I have, however, reflected since that, blinded by one pursuit, I badly missed out on what I might usefully and enjoyably have pursued elsewhere!

To conclude this digression I must say that when I started first to write this article, several months before the time I am writing now, I intended to finish with guesses, from the Luxembourg bus timetable, and 1:20,000 maps, as to descriptions of where I imagined I might be able to travel on the Weber double-decker, the inner stretches of which I had certainly done on local Luxembourg buses and some of the outer probably on the railway, thus a mixture of factual and emotional state of mind...

Fate or fortune favoured otherwise, and here in 2011 was I back, under the red, white and light blue horizontals of the flag. I could not resist, for commencement, a major hunt of the tri-partites or *double-accordeons*. I set out to one terminus of their route, 16, which I had not attempted hitherto, a place called Um Schlass, which, translated from Letzeburg tongue, means 'by the castle', a title which had fascinated me, but was actually an estate of well-heeled residences which the tripartites tackled by an exciting series of right-angle bends forming the terminal loop. While thus engaged I saw six tripartites in succession, in several varieties, out of the eight vehicles I believe are required to work the timetable; obviously an irresistible charm.

I then, however, repaired to the Rue Heine and the Rose Garden... to find, however, not a trace of a Weber double-decker. I made enquiries of a Weber driver

Vandivinit's double-decker escapes before the author can catch up with it...

on layover, in my best French, but he admitted he could speak only German, so I tried my best German, to which he replied he had been driving for Weber only a fortnight. I wished him luck in his new career and tried the next driver, one who could, unlike the first, speak French, and, after trying to fob me off with the green double-decker, a Weber two-axle tourist sightseeing vehicle with convertible roof not at all to my fancy, finally understood the purport of my search and said I should find one in the evening on the route to Trier, a well-patronised peak-hour service; but, especially on an autumn evening, perhaps somewhat tardy for my intentions.

Having studied Weber's addresses in the timetable and deciding that the Luxembourg premises sounded too touristy and that I would again be presented with the green beast, I elected for the main headquarters of Canach, despite the fact that on the 1:20,000 map it appeared – several kilometres outside the city – a totally rustic village, and accordingly set out thither on a common two-axle Weber single-decker. Its driver told me the *double-accordeons* had a reputation for breakdowns.

The route, after the not-unimpressive but familiarity-breeds-contempt section of the Boulevard Kennedy through the EU buildings and other modernity, proved, once in the country, to be extremely pretty with now and then wide views over

... although he did catch it later outside a building whose name translates as 'The shell'.

fine hills, and apple trees along the roadside with hundreds of apples lying on the verges. Was anyone going to pick them up?

Canach, flanked by a few active fields of vines and numerous fascinating hillside terraces of abandoned vineyards, was such a village as a few decades ago would have boasted dung heaps in the farmyards and runner-bean poles and cabbages in the cottage gardens. Now every farmyard and garden claimed an infill of ideal homes, the entire village was trimly bourgeois, and plainly a dormitory for the city. Half a mile beyond, amidst green fields, making me wonder about Luxembourg planning laws, was Weber's vast new though not uncomely bus depot, works and parking ground. Tucked in a corner of the yard was a three-axle double-decker, which, instinctively, I felt looked sad, though at that moment I had not learnt how old they might be.

A thoroughly urban secretary-bird, on hearing my mission, hastily led me through to an office of as familiar air as I could well imagine, screens humming, orders pinned up on boards or lying on desks. The bespectacled chap who most civilly answered my quest gave me a print-out of the evening timetable to Trier, duly marked with the two double-deck runs, (he said there were only two double-deckers) and a warning (which I thought on subsequent examination was false) that I might not get back on the last one to Luxembourg. He either could not, because he may not actually have known, or would not, because he did not wish to waste more time on the question, tell me where the two buses were in the afternoon... As I walked back towards the village of Canach first one and then the other of the double-decker three-axles thundered past me, one flying a schools yellow square, the other in all probability returning from a like task. What price now the third bus at the back of the yard?

Back on the Boulevard Kennedy, near the EU towers another (or presumably one of those two) thundered past me again, with the irritating destination screen 'Voyages Emile Weber' which may be translated 'sorry, not on service'. Later I saw one and then the other heading out for Trier, but the shades of night were falling fast and I did not especially desire to travel on a probably very full bus on a route much of which I knew and the rest of which I chose to guess might be equally unexciting.

Then, of an evening, I caught sight, from the balcony of the flat where I was staying, of a new star heading in a Thionville direction. In the latest mustard and blue livery of Voyages Vandivinit (if not as large an operator as Weber, quite a major player none the less) was a thoroughly modern three-axle double-decker, and definitely a bus rather than a coach. I saw it again, next day, about midday, coming in, and another sighting near the Gare enabled me to establish its route and its timing... the fly in the ointment being that the following day this working and two or three subsequent were all single-deckers, though I passed the intervening times agreeably

Swiss Postal delight, against the splendid art noveau background of St. Gallen railway station.

enough in a tavern where smoking was still allowed, and decorated on the outside with fin-de-siecle goddesses. Then at last, when I was walking home, the brute overtook me, stopped at a stop ahead just too far for me (too old to run for buses) to reach in time, shut its doors and shot off. The route to Thionville, I consoled myself, anyway, as I had been told and as I had seen from the railway, was of scant merit...

But it was at that moment that I decided that Fate had decreed that I was not intended to travel on Luxembourg three-axle double-deckers. Instead I achieved that which I had long desired – from map and timetable – to travel the whole south-eastern border of the Grand Duchy by the banks of the rivers Sure and Moselle, from Vianden via Echternach and Wasserbillig to Remich, over two days... all on single-deckers... even if some of them were three-axle...

Yes, I had abandoned the notion of three-axle double-decker travel in Luxembourg, but perhaps – we can always dream – the fool should return instead to his folly in St. Gallen...

West Midlands PTE:
then and now

Turning into Hill Street from Navigation Street on 10 November 1976, directly above the platforms at the western end of New Street station, is a former Birmingham City Transport standard Guy Arab IV/Metro-Cammell on the West Midland PTE's cross-city service 15 from Hamstead to Yardley, Whittington Oval. Operating the same service in the opposite direction is a sister vehicle from the same batch of 100 buses new in 1950/51. It is following a 1975 Daimler Fleetline/Park Royal.

Comparing photographs of the same location taken many years apart can be fascinating. A large number of publications now cover this subject but most seem to feature railways or general views in a particular locality although, more recently, a few have covered buses.

In a first for *Buses Yearbook*, I have selected a number of monochrome photographs I took in the late 1970s of West Midlands PTE buses and then, in January and February 2012, taken equivalent colour views at the same locations.

With the original pictures to hand for reference, where practicable I have taken the present-day

JOHN ROBINSON retraces his steps in the West Midlands in 2012, trying to replicate views taken more than 30 years earlier.

Captions by JOHN ROBINSON

photographs with the same focal length of lens from what I believe to be exactly the same position as the original. This is actually quite simple to achieve, by ensuring that all intersecting angles, such as rooflines, chimneys and windows appear in exactly the same relative positions in each pair of photographs. However, in some cases, I've shot slightly wider than originally in order to put the location in context or improve composition.

A lot of 'then and now' photographs featured in publications are frustratingly taken from different positions, even though the option to stand in exactly the same spot was available. By going the extra

NOW

THEN

The same location was still instantly recognisable when a National Express West Midlands (NXWM) Wrightbus Gemini-bodied Volvo B7TL was photographed on 8 January 2012, although it is undergoing major transformation as part of the Birmingham Gateway project to regenerate New Street station. This will see the extension of the Midland Metro tram route from Snow Hill to New Street station. As part of this work, buses ceased using this section of road from July 2012.

mile – or, more accurately, only a few footsteps in the required direction – the desired effect can be achieved and the comparison has the maximum visual impact.

The original photographs were taken with film cameras using prime lenses of either 50mm (standard) or 135mm (short telephoto) so it has been easy to replicate the same settings for the modern day pictures, taken with a digital camera.

I have featured locations where there are common elements in both pictures; if a location has completely changed beyond recognition with not even a single reference point to link it to the past view it would be difficult, if not impossible, to determine or access the spot the original picture was taken from and, even if this was possible, without any linking features the impact of a comparison shot would be lost.

The choice of views was largely dictated by the availability of suitable historic images so is not intended to reflect a broad spread of vehicle types or locations within the PTE's operating area. Regrettably, in those days, most of my photographs were record shots of the vehicles themselves, so placing the bus in

the context of its surroundings was only occasionally considered when taking the picture.

The pictures broadly start in Birmingham city centre and work outwards to the farthest location featured, Coventry.

It is clear that some locations have changed significantly more than others. What has changed in all the views, of course, are the buses themselves plus other vehicles and, in many cases, street furniture has become more visible. High street businesses have also changed and, importantly from a social perspective, fashions, including clothing.

Some of the shots I had intended to replicate were found to be no longer feasible when I re-visited the site. For example, the traditional Coventry shot in Broadgate with the half-timbered building in the background is no longer possible because it was in the process of being pedestrianised in February 2012, whilst part of Eagle Lane, Great Bridge, where I took a picture of an ex-West Bromwich Daimler Fleetline crossing the canal bridge in 1978 is now just a footpath.

THEN

NOW

Left: **One of the first batch of PTE standard Park Royal-bodied Daimler Fleetlines, new in 1971, negotiates St. Chads Circus Queensway on 29 June 1979 operating cross-city service 16, also from Hamstead to Yardley, Whittington Oval. Constitution Hill, the main road to West Bromwich and beyond, can be seen in the top centre of the picture curving round to the left. The city's Inner Ring Road tunnels under this spot; the light-coloured building on the left, behind the bushes in the roundabout, is part of the ventilation system. For a while the PTE continued the Birmingham City Transport practice of painting bus roofs khaki, as demonstrated here.**

Below left: **The road layout has changed considerably at this location with the pedestrian underpasses removed, bringing pedestrians back onto street level. Much of the background is still clearly identifiable despite new developments, and the ventilation building is now fully visible. The angle of approach of buses, together with an obstructing lamp post, necessitated a slightly different viewpoint to catch this NXWM TransBus-bodied Dennis Trident arriving on the 126 from Wolverhampton on 5 February 2012, although on this occasion the bus negotiated the junction using almost the same path as in the original picture. Service 126 was operated by Midland Red until the PTE acquired that operator's Birmingham and Black Country areas in December 1973.**

A former Coventry City Transport Deansgate-bodied Ford Transit 12-seat minibus, new in 1973, is seen in WMPTE ownership in Carrs Lane on 27 June 1979. On the edge of the picture on the right can be seen Carrs Lane Church Centre, located at the junction with Moor Street Queensway. Built of engineering bricks to reflect the industrial city, it was completed in 1970. Behind, a Metro-Cammell-bodied Leyland Fleetline loads for Chelmsley Wood South operating service 97.

On 5 February 2012 an NXWM Alexander Dennis Enviro400 pulls into the service 51 stop as it arrives from Walsall. The location is recognisable although a Travelodge with a Tesco Express below occupies the site of the building that was behind the Fleetline. The area of open land between this and the church is still present. In July 2012 the traffic flow in this street was reversed, meaning this view can no longer be captured.

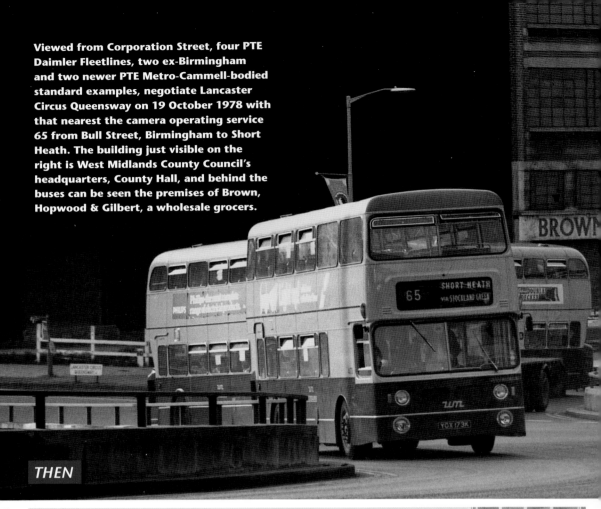

Viewed from Corporation Street, four PTE Daimler Fleetlines, two ex-Birmingham and two newer PTE Metro-Cammell-bodied standard examples, negotiate Lancaster Circus Queensway on 19 October 1978 with that nearest the camera operating service 65 from Bull Street, Birmingham to Short Heath. The building just visible on the right is West Midlands County Council's headquarters, County Hall, and behind the buses can be seen the premises of Brown, Hopwood & Gilbert, a wholesale grocers.

THEN

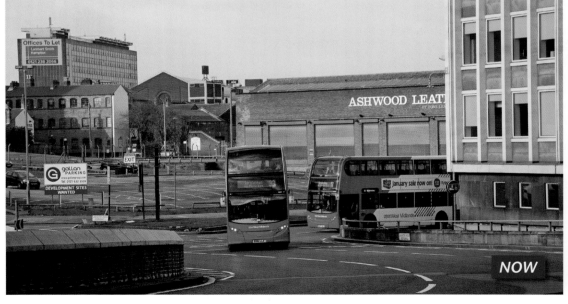

NOW

Another view of Lancaster Circus Queensway, seen from Newtown Row in May 1977 as a former Midland Red BMMO D9, dating from 1960, operates service 111 from the Bull Ring bus station to Roughley, a location just to the north of Sutton Coldfield. Dominating the background is Birmingham General Hospital and the flyover linking Corporation Street with St. Chads Queensway. The tower on the left is part of the Central Methodist Hall in Corporation Street.

Left: **The warehouse has now gone, opening up a view of the skyline, but the location is still recognisable as two NXWM Alexander Dennis Enviro400s head into the city centre on 22 January 2012 operating services 33 and 51 respectively. The two Lancaster Circus Queensway street name signs appear to be the originals whilst the former County Hall is now occupied by Birmingham City Council, although not as its headquarters. The office block which has become visible in the left distance is Centro House at 19 Summer Lane, the former headquarters of West Midlands PTE, displaying a large 'Offices To Let' banner.**

The scene is still instantly recognisable as a Scania OmniCity in the NXWM fleet heads out to Sutton Coldfield on 22 January 2012 operating service 904, with the background unchanged apart from an additional building on the extreme right at the hospital, which is now the Birmingham Children's Hospital. The wall of the roundabout has been rebuilt the solitary tree has grown significantly over the intervening 35 years, and now partially obscures the flyover.

THEN

NOW

Above: **Birmingham's iconic Rotunda dominates the skyline as one of the PTE's 1975 Daimler Fleetlines with Park Royal body heads out of the city centre along Digbeth on 13 October 1976, operating former Midland Red service 163 to Chelmsley Wood South. Chelmsley Wood, developed in the 1960s, was outside the city boundary so wasn't served by Birmingham City Transport, a position which was respected by the PTE until the takeover of Midland Red. Not long after this picture was taken the 163 was swallowed up into the 97/98 services. One of Digbeth's most recognisable buildings, the former Bonser & Co. warehouse, built in the 1860s for the firm of iron merchants, is the tower-like structure behind the bus. Just visible on the extreme right is part of Digbeth Civic Hall whilst the Mini, on the left, is turning into Rea Street on which the vehicle entrance to Digbeth Coach Station is located, just out of view.**

Below: **The location remains essentially unchanged in the current view taken on 22 January 2012 although the new icon of the Selfridges building is an additional feature. Clad in 15,000 shiny aluminium discs, its design was inspired by a Paco Rabanne sequinned dress. Surprisingly, the streetlamps appear not to have changed, that behind the bus being used to line up the picture with the original, although the tree has gone and railings have been installed on the pavements. Bonser's warehouse still stands although part of the 'Iron Warehouse' wording, cast in concrete, has broken off whilst the Old Bulls Head public house is now an Irish bar called the Kerryman. Co-incidentally, a BMW-built new-generation Mini waits to turn into Rea Street, just as in the original view, as an Alexander-bodied Dennis Trident, in an old NXWM livery, heads out to Cranes Park on service 60 with a TransBus-bodied Trident following on the 957 Limited Stop service to Solihull Station.**

THEN

The area around Digbeth and Deritend was the first centre of industry in Birmingham and became one of the most heavily industrialised areas in the town (it was not until 1889 that city status was granted, by Queen Victoria). This was in part due to Henry Bradford who, in 1767, donated land on Bradford Street to anyone willing to establish a trade there. Climbing out of the city along this street on service 50 to Maypole on 2 February 1979 is a 1963 Park Royal-bodied Daimler Fleetline from Birmingham's first large order for the type. It is just about to cross the junction with Alcester Street.

NOW

On 22 January 2012 the Selfridges building can be clearly seen but apart from this, and the loss of the factory chimneys behind the Fleetline, the skyline is essentially the same. The closest building, occupied by automotive component supplier Partco in the original picture, lies empty, whilst the junction with Alcester Street is now controlled by traffic lights. An NXWM Alexander Dennis Enviro400 passes, also operating service 50, now extended from Maypole to Druids Heath. Looking towards the city centre, the spire of St. Martin in the Bull Ring church can be seen to the left of the Rotunda.

Although Wednesbury had a bus station, there were also a number of street loading points scattered throughout the town centre. One of these, Ridding Lane, plays host to a 1969 ex-West Bromwich Daimler Fleetline/ECW on 22 June 1978 which had arrived on service 411 from its home town. To distinguish the lowheight bodywork on these from normal height double-deckers they wore what was effectively the single-deck livery with shallow blue skirts. Note the splendid old bus shelter, albeit in a somewhat dilapidated condition.

THEN

NOW

On 5 February 2012, following an overnight snowfall, an NXWM Mercedes-Benz 0405N passes by, operating service 410 en route from Wednesbury bus station to West Bromwich. Buses now stop at a modern shelter slightly further along Ridding Lane, out of shot, and although part of the building behind the bus has disappeared, those remaining are little changed, apart from having been modernised.

THEN

Left: **WMPTE was the first operator to place an MCW Metrobus in service. Climbing through Washwood Heath is 6831 (SDA 831S), the very first, part of a batch of five new in 1978 which were forerunners of an eventual fleet of 1,130. It is passing its home depot, just out of sight on the right of the picture, on 21 June 1978 on service 93 from Kingshurst to its City Centre terminus in Bull Street. The Metro-Cammell-Weymann factory in Common Lane, where the bus was built, is just a stone's throw away, beyond the properties on the left. No doubt the proximity of the builder to the depot, should any technical issues arise, was considered advantageous.**

Right: **On 5 February 2012 an NXWM Alexander-bodied Volvo B7TL operates service 94 from Chelmsley Wood. The location is relatively unchanged although the nearest phone box has gone and a speed camera installed outside the site of Washwood Heath bus depot, now occupied by a large supermarket. The car lot has also gone, along with the hedges in front of the nearest properties. Both the 93 and 94 services were created in the PTE's first big round of rationalisation of former Birmingham City Transport and Midland Red services in November 1975.**

NOW

THEN

Left: **A number of former Coventry Metro-Cammell-bodied Daimler CVG6s were transferred by the PTE to Birmingham for operation on the Outer Circle, which remained crew-operated until March 1978 when such operation from Birmingham depots finished. This Daimler, new in 1958, negotiates the Birchfield Road roundabout in Perry Barr as it crosses from Wellington Road to Aston Lane operating an 11C on 7 February 1977.**

Right: **The present view is virtually unchanged, although the block in the background has been re-glazed and the shops changed hands, as one of NXWM's Wrightbus Gemini-bodied Volvo B7TLs makes the same manoeuvre on 8 January 2012.**

NOW

THEN

Above: **Coventry was the last outpost of traditional front-engined buses in the PTE, the final ones being withdrawn in 1979. Waiting at the traffic lights in Fairfax Street on 6 July 1977 are two Metro-Cammell-bodied Daimler CVG6s, that on the left still wearing Coventry's red and ivory livery while the bus on the right is in PTE colours. The 'H' above the driver's window denotes their allocation to Harnall Lane East, one of two PTE depots in the city, both now replaced by one in Wheatley Street close to Pool Meadow bus station. The latter is located beyond the shop frontages on the left of the picture. The De Vere Hotel, which straddles Fairfax Street, looms large in the background whilst the building on the right is a multi-storey car park with shops at street level.**

Left: **This area has seen extensive redevelopment and is now called Millennium Place. Although the De Vere has become the Britannia Coventry Hotel it is otherwise the only unchanged feature visible. The present view is taken from slightly closer to the hotel as it was not possible to stand in exactly the same position. It was also necessary to work around the proliferation of street furniture to obtain this picture of a De Courcey, Coventry, ex-West Midlands MCW Metrobus, new in 1983, heading out of the city to take up school bus duties on 2 February 2012.**

Bus Rapid Transit

Bus Rapid Transit has had a chequered history in the UK, but that may be changing, as *Buses* editor **ALAN MILLAR** explains.

All pictures by author except where stated otherwise.

An Alexander Dennis Enviro400-bodied Scania N230UB of Stagecoach East at speed on The Busway, which connects St. Ives with Cambridge.

For decades, the words 'bus' and 'rapid transit' seemed like opposites in the lexicon of public transport.

Trams, light railways, metro trains and other manifestations of steel wheels on steel rails were deemed essential for mass movements of people to be achieved at relatively high speed in urban areas. Buses were, well, just buses; comparatively slow-moving, unfashionable vehicles carrying people where fancy fast trains and their ilk could not go or did not yet go.

So it was that after the last of Britain's first generation of tramways closed in the 1950s and early 1960s, city transport planners began plotting their revival as rapid transit. Tyneside eventually got its Metro. Manchester tried to get Picc-Vic, an ambitious scheme to connect suburban railways through a city centre tunnel, and instead by the early 1990s began uniting them as Metrolink, a city centre tramway that extended to outer suburbs and surrounding towns along converted heavy rail track.

It began to look like no city could contemplate future existence, let alone future public transport, without something similar. Sheffield built Supertram, Birmingham and Wolverhampton were connected by a tram-cum-light railway called Midland Metro, London built both the Docklands Light Railway and Croydon Tramlink, the latter – like Manchester's tramway – connecting underused and reopened heavy railways with street-running trams.

Nottingham followed all this with NET – Nottingham Express Transit – which was developed effectively as a rail-based version of the city's otherwise bus-served high-frequency transport corridors.

All these cities dreamed of expanding their first lines into more comprehensive networks, while plans were advanced for similar systems elsewhere, including Bristol, Leeds, Liverpool, Glasgow, Edinburgh, South Hampshire (Portsmouth and its surroundings) and a good many smaller places, too, like Preston for example.

When first elected, the 1997 Labour government talked of approving one new light rail scheme a year as part of a plan to encourage far more of us to switch to public transport, but its enthusiasm waned as it became apparent not only that rail-based rapid transit projects are costly and hugely disruptive to install, but seem prone to construction delays and cost over-runs on a disturbing scale.

Within nine years, approval was withdrawn for several tramways that had looked as though they

would have gone ahead, and the message filtering out to local transport authorities was to look seriously at the bus-based alternative, BRT.

The reassurance of permanence

One of trams' great selling points is that the system looks permanent and – when seen through the eyes of those unfamiliar with public transport – easy to use. The vehicles will only run where there are rails and stop only at stations or halts. Another is that because they have their own track, other road users keep clear of them or are kept clear so trams whisk ahead of slower-moving traffic.

The high cost of construction is partly because underground services – water pipes, gas mains, electricity cables – need to be relocated away from where heavy trams could damage them. Moving them may also expose problems with the foundations of neighbouring buildings.

And the cost means that trams and their ilk are best suited to where the heaviest flows of people need to be transported: big cities with closely-packed apartments and lots of commercial activity. If they are also to serve areas of low-density housing, then passengers may need to transfer on to a connecting feeder bus or the promoters of the project bear the risk that even a sleek, shiny, sexy tram may not generate sufficient traffic to justify the expenditure.

Transport planners in past decades seemed not to worry unduly about this. Rather like their

Sheffield Supertram cost £240million to build and opened in 1994/95 with a fleet of 25 German-built Siemens-Duewag trams. Stagecoach has operated it since 1997.

colleagues in town planning who saw high-rise tower blocks as a solution for urban living – but probably bought themselves suburban or rural houses with ground-level access to private gardens – they saw nothing wrong in bus/rail interchanges for relatively short public transport journeys. Indeed, they promoted them as a Good Thing, a component part of integrated public transport.

If some of those planners inhabited an unreal, theoretical world in which these arrangements looked good on paper – especially when illustrated with drawings in which perfect families and their 2.4 children stride through urban landscapes bathed in Mediterranean sunshine and unvandalised public architecture – real passengers saw things differently.

Forced interchanges were an inconvenience that added uncertainty to a journey (would the connection be there?), discomfort (more wind and rain than Mediterranean sun), perceived danger (unsavoury,

A Wrightbus Pulsar 2-bodied VDL SB200 of Arriva North West pulling away from a typically utilitarian bus shelter on the Runcorn Busway. It is heading for Halton Lea, the new name for what originally was called Runcorn Shopping City. GARY MITCHELHILL

threatening people loitering around looking nothing like the perfect families in the drawings) and the plain nuisance of an interruption partway through a relatively short journey.

If you could have a system that combines the permanence, reassurance and exclusive track of light rail with buses' ability to serve low density housing without interchanges, then it could often be a more attractive solution for users.

With BRT, the exclusive track may be confined to the main trunk section or perhaps only to pinch points where it speeds buses past slow-moving general traffic, and buses can fan out and run beyond the reserved roads to serve the places hard or impossible to reach with trams.

The Runcorn Busway

BRT came to the UK a long time before anyone used the term. This was the Runcorn Busway, a 22km

A symptom of the neglect that has afflicted the Runcorn Busway in the decades since its royal opening. In April 2009, caravans and gas canisters blocked one of its access roads. MICHAEL JONES

A Wrightbus Eclipse Urban-bodied Volvo B7RLE of First West Yorkshire entering one of the sections of guided busway in Leeds.

A Metrobus Scania OmniCity on a section of Fastway guided busway in the centre reservation of London Road, Crawley. METROBUS

(13.7mile) bus-only circle and branches opened in 1973 to provide local public transport within a five-minute walk of 90% of the population of this, one of the later new towns built in a postwar programme to accommodate a dispersed and growing population.

There had been talk of futuristic public transport – think monorails and moving pavements – in new towns. But Runcorn was the only one built with such an extensive dedicated track, on which NBC's Crosville provided services with contemporary single-deckers like the Seddon Pennine RU and Leyland National; even a unique battery electric example of the latter.

It was a showpiece that merited a royal opening – by the Queen – and might have led to more such facilities had the building of new towns not been grinding to a halt. Short stretches of dedicated busway also were built in the new towns of Redditch and Irvine, but on nothing like the scale of Runcorn.

Two things let down the Runcorn Busway. One was the fact that, good as it was at whisking residents to and from the main shopping centre, it offered no great benefit over driving there by car. The planners made sure that, like other new towns, they gave Runcorn a top class urban highway system on which residents could drive almost anywhere with ease.

The second drawback may partly be a consequence of that first one. It is that the infrastructure – the track and especially the bus stops and shelters – became neglected. What had been intended as a quality public transport facility took on the down-at-heel appearance of all too many bus routes on public roads. It looked unappealing and a place to avoid rather than use.

Nearly 40 years after it opened, it is still in use, served by Arriva and Halton buses. But it serves as a warning that like puppies at Christmas, investment in grand projects is a lifetime commitment. They must be kept attractive long after the official opening.

Guidance revives interest

Interest in BRT revived towards the end of the 1980s with the arrival of an added ingredient: the kerb-guided bus. First installed in the German city of Essen in 1980 and then more extensively in Adelaide, South Australia in 1986-89, this gives buses some of the characteristics of a tram or train by allowing the track rather than the driver to steer it.

Arriva Southern Counties operates the two Fastrack services with a dedicated fleet of Wrightbus-bodied Volvo B7RLEs. JAMES EXCELL

The Fastlink guided busway in Edinburgh, next to the railway towards Glasgow. The Wrightbus Eclipse Urban-bodied Volvo B7RLE is operating a route that may one day be replaced by trams. GARY MITCHELHILL

Close up view of a guidewheel on a First bus.

Small wheels are mounted horizontally on arms attached to the steering axle. These arms fit into the upper edges of the raised concrete kerb alongside the track and steer the vehicle. In turn, that means the bus can be confined within a narrower space than if a human steers it, and it can be driven at relatively high speed.

Unlike a tram, a bus is comparatively light, so there is much less need to divert underground services from beneath the track.

It also is possible to have optically guided buses, using cameras to follow lines painted on the road surface, or electronic guidance with cables buried just below the road surface. These systems make it possible to guide buses through city centre streets without pedestrians and cyclists tripping over the raised sections of track, but the technology – tried mainly in France – has yet to prove itself to be practical and trouble-free.

The first UK demonstration of kerb-guided buses was in Birmingham in 1984 where a 600m stretch of suburban track was installed and a small fleet of MCW Metrobus double-deckers was built to use it. The experiment lasted only a couple of years but the idea slowly took root. A 500m guided busway opened in Ipswich in 1994, four sections totalling 1.5km opened the following year on Scott Hall Road in Leeds, followed in 2001 by three sections totalling 2km on the city's York Road.

The Leeds guideways proved the point about benefits to be gained from concentrating scarce infrastructure funds on pinch points where buses could get past queues of general traffic – some are one-way tracks – but hardly were rapid transit in the meaning of the Act.

Crawley Fastway was a more complete BRT project. This scheme, connecting parts of the West Sussex new town with the adjacent Gatwick Airport, opened in sections from 2004 and used 1.5km of guided and 8.8km of unguided bus lanes to provide a higher quality service along key corridors.

The buses – Scania OmniCity single-deckers operated by Go-Ahead's Metrobus subsidiary – are painted in a blue and silver Fastway livery. Bus stops have smart shelters with real-time information. Traffic light priorities, road realignment and barrier-controlled bus-only roads help make the service run more smoothly than a conventional bus route.

However, it suffered from delays and cost over-runs – from a budgeted £27million to over £35million – and ended up being scaled back from original intentions. Such problems clearly are not confined to

A TransBus-bodied Volvo B7TL of First Eastern Counties on the short stretch of guided busway at Kesgrave, Ipswich. GARY MITCHELHILL

trams, though the sums involved are smaller.

It was followed in 2006/07 by Fastrack – a trend was developing on names for British BRT lines – serving north Kent. Two lines, neither of them guided but both benefiting from substantial sections of dedicated track and high-quality stops, connected Dartford and Gravesend with major facilities including Ebbsfleet railway station on the high-speed Channel Tunnel link and Bluewater shopping centre.

It was part-funded by the developer of The Bridge, a huge brownfield site being transformed into a combination of residential and commercial properties, and was installed before many of these were ready. The idea was to establish public transport as a viable option from the start and live Fastrack information was fed into some of the new houses.

Arriva operated Fastrack with Wrightbus-bodied Volvo B7RLEs in a distinctive blue and grey livery.

Another project with a similar name –Fastlink – opened in Edinburgh in 2004. This was a 1.5km guideway paralleling a stretch of railway on the city's western approaches, which was less significant for what it was than what it might have been and what it led towards.

It was retrieved from a far more grand scheme, abandoned in 2001, called City of Edinburgh Rapid Transit (Cert), a guided busway linking the city centre with Edinburgh Airport by way of a major suburban commercial development. Cert got so far as the selection of a consortium to build and run it, which included FirstGroup as the operating partner, but fell apart when serious doubts arose over its viability.

Cert was budgeted to cost £50million to build, whereas Fastlink cost £10million. It closed towards the end of 2008 ready for conversion into a tramway as part of an intended £545million 12mile cross-city route due to open in 2011.

The tramway may now open in 2014, has been scaled back to 7miles ending in the city centre and will cost around £1billion. The Edinburgh tram project killed off that city's token stretch of BRT, but its cost over-runs and delays may have advanced the case elsewhere for BRT over rail-based rapid transit.

The future looked like StreetCar

First may have helped pull the plug on Cert, but in September 2004 in a move to focus local transport authorities' minds on the BRT alternative as cherished tram projects hit the buffers of government rejection, it previewed an articulated bus disguised as a modern tram.

This was the Wrightbus StreetCar, based on a modified Volvo B7LA chassis with the front axle moved ahead of the front door, under the driver's cab, which was sealed off from the passenger saloon. The body was taller than a conventional single-decker and the front was encased in a sleek nose cone.

This was about more than the StreetCar. It would operate alongside the whole panoply of BRT infrastructure – tram-like stops, reserved track, traffic light priorities and off-bus or self-service fare

A StreetCar leading a Plaxton Pointer-bodied Dennis Dart SLF of First Cymru through part of the two-way busway created in central Swansea as part of the 'ftr' Metro project.

Swansea Metro uses the city's Landore busway, built between the main line railway and modern housing and accessed by electric gates.

collection. The whole package came with a name – 'ftr', text shorthand for 'future' – and other language that smacked of a bus denying it was a bus. Its drivers were 'pilots' who sat in a 'cockpit'.

First's then chief executive, the yet-to-be-knighted Moir Lockhead, declared: "Quite simply, we've torn up the local transport textbook to start over again." The group's message was that if cities wanted StreetCars, they must sign up to provide the accompanying infrastructure.

A prototype bus was unveiled the following March and 39 more were ordered in time for the first 'ftr' line opening in York in May 2006. But the StreetCar cart was provided before the 'ftr' horse. York got BRT buses without BRT.

A partnership with the city council saw a stretch of road through a housing estate resurfaced and provided with off-street parking to make way for the buses, but there was no new reserved track.

Worse than that, there was no dress rehearsal of the self-service ticket machines installed on the buses' front platforms. Far from speeding up the service, they slowed it horribly as passengers queued out into the street waiting their turn to use them. StreetCars bunched and gaps opened up in the

schedule. Conductors (or 'customer service hosts' if you please) were recruited to collect fares.

First's haste to get these expensive assets out earning saw a route converted gradually to StreetCars in Leeds, with conductors aboard from the outset and infrastructure investment confined largely to painting bigger 'no parking' bays at stops. A few others were deployed at Luton Airport on the shuttle service to the Parkway railway station.

The Luton fleet and others, which were mothballed until needed, went on to the one 'ftr' project worthy of the name: Swansea Metro, which was phased into use during 2009. Swansea Council invested in infrastructure improvements, notably in the centre where half a dual carriageway was converted into a two-way busway.

By then, First's enthusiasm had evaporated. Employing conductors increased labour costs and the heavy StreetCars were formidable gas guzzlers. To reduce costs, conventional buses – Dennis Darts in Swansea – took their place at weekends and Sundays.

Although Wright Group exported hybrid electric StreetCars to Las Vegas, First has bought no more for the UK and the biggest sign that the sun had set on this project came early in 2012 when First agreed to withdraw the original fleet from York, where a change of governing party had killed the council's previous enthusiasm for 'ftr'.

Following major refurbishment of their careworn interiors, they are being redeployed on a service between Leeds and Bradford.

Cambridgeshire provides the showpiece

BRT desperately needed a proper UK showpiece, which finally appeared in August 2011 with the delayed opening of The Busway, the world's longest – 25km (15.5mile) – guided busway on a 40km (25mile) interurban route between Cambridge and St. Ives. Having seen other schemes use about every imaginable word combination that included 'fast' but excluded 'bus, Cambridgeshire appears to prove that commuters are unafraid of the supposedly off-putting B-word.

This project has brought its own heartaches, opening over two years late and costing at least £30million more than the £150million originally agreed. The relationship between Cambridgeshire County Council, which commissioned it, and contractor BAM Nuttall (which also built Crawley Fastway) went into meltdown before it opened.

It was surrounded by controversy from the start because it was built on abandoned railway trackbed, which rail campaigners wanted to see reopened with passenger and freight trains. Those campaigners were relentless in criticising the very idea of guided buses.

While they might have provided longer distance connections, trains would not have penetrated Cambridge city centre in the way that the bus service does. The Victorian university authorities were determined that students should not be corrupted by the influences of the modern world that they imagined the railway would bring to their city, so the station is a good mile south-east of the centre.

The Busway has two separate sections of guideway, the main stretch from St. Ives into the north of Cambridge, with a short connecting stretch of unguided busway through a new housing development, and a shorter section south from the railway station to a park-and-ride at Trumpington. In between, buses use public roads – some but by no means all with bus priorities – to cross the city centre.

The service through the city is subject to unpredictable delays, but the upside is that it takes people where they want to go. With two operators – Stagecoach mainly, but also Whippet Coaches – running an offpeak daytime service at least every 10 minuntes, it also is more frequent than would have been possible by rail.

The southernmost section of The Busway in Cambridge is single track to pass through narrow railway arches. This is a Wrightbus Eclipse 2-bodied Volvo B7RLE of Stagecoach East.

First operates the South Hants Eclipse service with Wrightbus-bodied Volvo B7RLEs.

The guideway sections allow buses to reach surprisingly high speeds between stops, which generally are built to – and hopefully maintained to – as high a standard as one would expect of light rail.

It carried nearly 56,000 passengers over its first seven days and its millionth in just over five months. Cambridgeshire hopes it will be carrying 11,500 a day by the end of its first year.

There will be another one behind

Like the old cliché about buses, suddenly a whole bunch of BRT schemes is coming in the wake of The Busway.

Eclipse is the name chosen for the South Hants scheme being built in place of a tramway deemed too expensive, with the initial Gosport-Fareham section opening in spring 2012 on a former railway trackbed. It has much of the appearance of The Busway, but without guided buses. First operates the service using 12m Wrightbus-bodied Volvo B7RLEs in a special livery.

Guided busways are being built connecting Luton and Dunstable, and Leigh and Manchester, largely over abandoned railways. BRT projects have also gained approval for Bristol, South Yorkshire and East Lancashire, while the Scottish government is funding another project north of the border called Fastlink, this time an unguided route in Glasgow serving communities, commercial and social facilities either side of the River Clyde. This Fastlink may incorporate induction loops beneath the road surface to recharge the batteries of electric buses as they progress along the route.

There also are plans for BRT in Belfast, though these have been scaled back from one involving substantial sections of segregated track to ones making use of dedicated sections of public highways.

And as I write this, Leeds is waiting to find out if New Generation Transport (NGT), its scheme for trolleybus rapid transit on cross-city lines connecting park-and-ride car parks, will finally secure government approval and bring trolleybuses back to UK streets for the first time in over 40 years. Plans for more conventional BRT in Thurrock and Southend were also awaiting a government decision.

NGT was developed by Metro, the West Yorkshire PTE, after the UK government rejected an increasingly expensive Leeds Supertram.

One hurdle it has faced is that decision makers – ultimately HM Treasury – appear not to understand what trolleybuses are. They vanished from London half a century ago in May 1962 and fizzled out

View from the top of a Stagecoach double-decker as it prepares to leave the main highway to join a section of The Busway in the north of Cambridge.

An image showing Glasgow Fastlink, using half the carriageway of the Broomielaw close to the city centre. Although the artist envisages an articulated single-decker, it is more likely to use double-deckers or rigid single-deckers. STRATHCLYDE PARTNERSHIP FOR TRANSPORT

elsewhere within another 10 years. The chances are that the economists and senior civil servants have never knowingly clapped eyes on one.

This was apparent when a 1998 public inquiry rejected a plan for electronically guided BRT trolleybuses in Liverpool, the stumbling block being the inspector's reluctance to permit quiet electric vehicles in pedestrianised city streets.

Supporters of rail-based rapid transit will argue – with justification – that BRT may not carry such large numbers of passengers per hour as their favoured solution, but its steady acceptance in the UK shows it has an important role to play and that it is often the only affordable solution available when public funds are in short supply. Its day may have come.

Animal.
magic

Animals, or animal references, form the theme to a selection of photographs from **TONY WILSON**.

It is July 1993, and a Wilts & Dorset Optare MetroRider, new in 1992, gently eases its way around stubborn locals as they go at their own leisurely pace along the road leading into Burley in the New Forest. The ponies – or their successors – may well still be around, but the X1 service between Bournemouth and Southampton has been withdrawn.

One horse power versus 115bhp as a horse meets a London Transport RT-class AEC Regent III as it waits in the Kent village of Downe before setting off on the return run up to Bromley in May 1978.

Down into the village of Burley and in June 1982 a donkey gazes forlornly at a passing Hants & Dorset Leyland National in the National Bus Company's local coach livery. It is heading for Southampton on the same X1 service as the MetroRider shown opposite, and carries local South Wessex fleetnames.

Above: **To the east coast now and Scarborough promenade in July 1996, as the donkeys head towards the beach for their day's work. An ex-Greater Manchester Atlantean operated by Applebys waits for the donkeys to pass before continuing its duties on the seafront service.**

Below: **From seaside surroundings to the wide open spaces of the Peak District in Derbyshire, and high above Hathersage a Mainline Metrobus heads along the open road bound for Castleton in June 1994 on a service from Sheffield. The ruminant on the side of the road is so used to this sort of event that it took no notice of the bus or the photographer as it continued to munch on the grass.**

Left: **Into London now, and whilst animals might not be prolific, birds of a feather certainly are well in evidence. Here a Routemaster is seen in April 1999, pulling away from the bus station on the forecourt of Victoria Station and alarming a flock of pigeons on the ground.**

Middle: **The connection with animals is more obscure in this image from September 2001. It was the height of the last major outbreak of foot and mouth disease in the UK, and to prevent it spreading further, people and vehicles were strictly monitored in many areas of the countryside, and measures were taken by the authorities to ensure vehicles were disinfected at certain points. A new Wrightbus-bodied Volvo B10BLE from the Yorkshire-based Reliance company receives just such attention as it rests between duties on one of the summer Sunday services which made up part of the Moorsbus network.**

Below: **Inland in August 1979 and a service bus finds its progress halted at Goathland within the North Yorkshire Moors National Park, as some of the local residents face up to a dog. This 1968 West Yorkshire Road Car Bristol RE was heading from the Leeds area to Whitby.**

Moving away from actual wildlife, a flock of stylised sheep decorate the side of this Trent MAN with Optare Vecta bodywork. The bus is on one of a group of routes that served the communities between Derby and Burton-on-Trent and were branded under the 'Villager' name. The sheep and the hills on the side of the bus are designed to indicate the rural nature of the routes, although this bus is in decidedly urban Burton-on-Trent.

No immediate animal connection may be evident here, but a closer look into the destination of this Daimler Fleetline shows that London Buses subsidiary, London Northern, provided a link to and from London Zoo in August 1993. There's a stylised zebra head alongside the route information in the intermediate route display.

Bringing the subject up to date and Edinburgh Zoo was in the news in 2012 with the arrival of two Giant Pandas from China. For some while now a small number of buses on the route that passes the zoo have promoted it with a selection of wildlife images on the sides of various vehicles. All are Wrightbus Gemini-bodied Volvo B9TLs, as seen in Musselburgh in October 2009. A tiger encourages passengers to have a 'purrfect day out'.

And finally, a rather novel way of rounding up sheep perhaps. A Leyland Tiger from the small fleet of heritage vehicles operated by Cumbria Classic Coaches of Ravenstonedale near Kirkby Stephen, is held up by an errant gathering of locals.

The changing face of PMT

At the end of 1980 Potteries Motor Traction, better known as PMT, was just another National Bus Company subsidiary, with the mainstay of its fleet being standard NBC Bristol VRTs and REs with ECW bodywork, Leyland Nationals, and a handful of New Bus Grant coaches. All of these vehicles carried the obligatory poppy red and white livery, apart from a few all-over advert vehicles.

In October 1980 the last pre-NBC buses had been withdrawn on the implementation of service alterations as part of NBC's Market Analysis Project. This removed the last Alexander-bodied Daimler Fleetlines and PMT's original Leyland Atlanteans from the fleet, along with surviving AEC Reliances and Leyland Leopard service buses. Newer vehicles

CLIFF BEETON looks at the rise and fall of PMT over the 30 years from NBC to First.

All photographs by the author.

were not exempt from the fleet rationalisation either. Early Bristol REs left at the same time, as did a lot of short Leyland Nationals. Also leaving were the remaining conductors, as the fleet became 100% one-man operated.

A few unusual vehicles remained however, the most interesting being Alexander-bodied Dennis Dominator 700 (XBF 700S) and Foden NC 900 (WVT 900S). These two buses were allocated by NBC to PMT in 1978 as experimental vehicles to undertake comparative trials with standard Bristol VRT 686 (YBF 686S), which was renumbered 600 during the trials.

PMT also received more Bristol VRTs, then Leyland Olympians, National 2s and Plaxton-bodied

Leyland Tigers during the later NBC years before pioneering minibus operation using the Minilink brand in 1983 with its own home-built conversions of Mercedes-Benz, Ford Transit and later Leyland Sherpa vans. Large numbers of these entered the fleet, doubling frequencies on many routes but operated by drivers on lower rates of pay and different conditions of employment.

The Dominator was to leave for Maidstone & District in 1983, as that company had a batch of similar vehicles. The Foden lasted a little longer in service, but was always a troublesome vehicle and tended to be kept on the Newcastle - Tesco Trent Vale free bus service, because it was close to Newcastle garage in case of problems.

In 1983 rumours persisted that local independent operator, Berresfords of Cheddleton, along with associate company Stoniers of Goldenhill, were being closed down because they owed money to the Inland Revenue. To be able to operate replacement services at short notice if this happened, PMT acquired 13 Bristol REs of various vintages from the Bristol Omnibus Company. Eleven entered service; the other two were used for spares. All bar one of these had the earlier flat-screen version of the ECW body, a type never operated by PMT before. The irony here was that PMT had disposed of many newer examples only a few years earlier. Unusually they entered

Two Bristol LHS6Ls from National Welsh joined the PMT fleet in 1985. New in 1981, they had coach-seated ECW bodies. They were PMT's only LHs.

Second-hand Bristol REs from the Bristol Omnibus Co entered service in green with prominent PMT lettering on the front to reassure passengers looking for a red bus. This one is seen at Hanley Bus Station.

service in NBC green livery, with PMT fleetnames, and an additional PMT name on the front to reassure confused passengers. As they were seen as a short-term acquisition, the cost of a repaint into poppy red was not justified. Berresfords, however, kept on running, so the Bristol REs were deployed on normal PMT routes, with two eventually getting a coat of poppy red paint.

Another two interesting arrivals in the dying NBC years were a pair of Bristol LHs with ECW bodywork from National Welsh. These had manual gearboxes and were the only LHs ever to work for PMT.

In 1985 the Conservative government announced that the National Bus Company was to be privatised and, as a prelude to this, the previous tight centralised control on liveries was relaxed, with many companies expressing their new freedom with bold new colour schemes. As an experiment a Bristol

Above: **The livery used by the privatised PMT company was this bright combination of red and yellow. This ECW-bodied Olympian in Birkenhead is part of the Crosville fleet.**

Left: **The only Foden NC operated by the National Bus Company was allocated to the PMT fleet. It is seen here at Newcastle garage in NBC's corporate poppy red, the only livery it carried.**

For a short time Pennine buses were repainted in a blue and yellow version of PMT's livery, as seen on this ECW-bodied VRT which is operating on a PMT service in Stoke-on-Trent.

VR was painted in a darker red and yellow livery on the front and nearside. The offside and rear were painted in the same darker red, but with dark cream. It never went on the road in this scheme

When I told Steve Ellis, the managing director of PMT at the time, that the cream and red looked better than the red and yellow. He replied, "We are going forward not backwards!" From then on the red and yellow livery was adopted as standard, at first with red wheels, but soon reverting to NBC-style grey. The first repaints carried the NBC double-N symbol on the front. Most vehicles were repainted at PMT's Stoke Central Works, but some were done by Crosville at Chester.

PMT was purchased from NBC in a management buyout in October 1986 and was now a private company once again. The new company started to strengthen its hand by building its own bodywork on minibus and midibus chassis in preparation for deregulation, and also expanded its area of operation by opening a depot at Crewe to service a large amount of tendered work for Cheshire County Council, which it had won from Crosville. These tenders took PMT buses out as far as Macclesfield on a service from Crewe. Another new depot was at Moreton, on the Wirral peninsula, opened to operate tendered services for Merseytravel.

The services at Moreton were branded Red Rider instead of PMT, but retained the standard red and yellow livery. Another Red Rider base opened at Willenhall in the West Midlands, again operating tendered services, this time for the West Midlands PTE. The Willenhall base was eventually exchanged with Stevensons of Uttoxeter for their operations in

Stockport, but no vehicles changed hands.

The last remote base to open was in Leeds, but here a problem arose when PMT used the Red Rider name, for Yorkshire Rider, the main operator in the area, objected to its use, because it marketed many of its own routes using the Rider name, such as Gold Rider. It threatened court action, so PMT used the name Cityline instead. Only operating a handful of vehicles, the base at Leeds did not last too long.

The opening of these new depots increased the requirement for double-deckers, and many of PMT's own were given a second lease of life after being replaced by new vehicles. Second-hand Bristol VRTs were also acquired from South Midland and West Yorkshire.

In 1987 PMT started buying up the remaining independent operators in North Staffordshire. The first were Berresfords and Stoniers in April. At first they operated with no change, but they were soon closed down with only three Berresfords vehicles joining the PMT fleet. One was a former Trent Bristol RELH coach, which received red and yellow bus livery; the other two were Leyland Leopard coaches, which joined the Paramount Coaching department. An ex-Berresfords AEC Swift did work for PMT at Cheadle, but this was only for a short while, and it was not repainted into PMT colours.

In October 1987 Turners of Brown Edge was acquired, with five double-deckers (three Northern Counties-bodied Fleetlines and two youthful ex-West Yorkshire PTE Olympians with Roe bodies) and four coaches joining the PMT fleet. The Turners garage at Brown Edge continued to operate the ex-Turners routes for a few months but was eventually closed,

Two PMT Olympians were repainted in Turners livery, acknowledging the respect customers had for the former independent company. Only the alpha-numeric fleet number gives the clue that the bus is owned by PMT.

Among the more unusual buses to carry the standard livery were three-axle Olympians imported from Hong Kong and allocated to the Pennine business.

with the vehicles transferring to PMTs Hanley Clough Street garage. The two Roe-bodied Olympians were transferred to the Red Rider base at Stockport shortly afterwards and repainted red and yellow. They were highbridge vehicles, and with many low bridges in the Potteries it was thought too risky to keep them local. Two standard PMT low-height ECW Olympians received Turners livery to replace them. Turners buses were held in high esteem by passengers in the Potteries, consequently the Turners name and livery were to continue with PMT until the establishment of the FirstGroup corporate livery many years later.

In 1989, following five years of minibuses, midibuses and a few coaches joining the fleet, the first full-size vehicles arrived. These were ten Leyland Olympians with Leyland bodies. Three were bus-seated models; the other seven were coach-seated and six of these were in a stunning silver livery for operation between Hanley and Crewe. The seventh was red and yellow and was based at Cheadle for the X23 Hanley-Derby service. These were to be the last double-deckers purchased new

by PMT.

Attention then turned to evaluating demonstration vehicles before finalising an order for the company's first full-size single-deckers since the last Leyland National 2s, trying out a Leyland Lynx, Optare Delta, Wright-bodied Scania and even a Northern Counties-bodied Renault. The company eventually decided on 11 Leyland Lynxes and nine Optare Deltas. These were for main line route 24, Talke Pits to Meir Square, replacing Bristol VRTs.

As well as a large fleet of minibuses, a large coaching fleet of Leyland Tigers and Scanias, mainly with Plaxton bodywork, had been built up; it also included some older acquired Leyland Leopards and in 1989 was formed into a separate operation as Paramount Leisure, with the letters PMT in the ParaMounT name being painted red to identify the link with PMT.

A 1990 acquisition was Landliner Goldcrest of Birkenhead which operated minibuses, some of which joined PMT's Flexi minibus fleet. But by far the largest acquisition was when the remnants of Crosville on the Wirral peninsula were taken over

PMT built the body on this Leyland Swift. This style of body was called the Knype, the name writer Arnold Bennett used for Stoke in his Five Towns novels. Originally red and yellow, it is seen here in the livery used for PMT's Flexi buses.

from Drawlane, with 164 vehicles and the depots at Chester, Rock Ferry, Ellesmere Port and Birkenhead. The Crosville name was retained, and after initial thoughts of using a yellow and light green version of the PMT livery, it was eventually decided to use the standard red and yellow. Repaints in these colours soon started. Eventually the Red Rider operation at Moreton was integrated into the Crosville operation. Ultimately former Crosville vehicles started to be transferred into the main fleet, and instances of Crosville green and cream vehicles working in the Potteries occurred.

PMT eventually adopted the Crosville-style alpha-numeric fleet numbering system, but before this any ex-Crosville vehicle transferred to the main fleet gained the prefix number 2 or 3 added to its fleet number. For example KFM125Y was Crosville's DOG125 but became 2125 when working in the Potteries. Leyland National EFM 323S was SNG 325 but became 3325 on transfer to Hanley.

The Birkenhead operations of C&M of Aintree joined the ever-expanding PMT group in 1992. Three minibuses were taken into PMT stock.

Up to this time most midibuses in the PMT fleet were bodied in house: Mercedes-Benz with PMT Ami bodywork and Leyland Swifts with the angular PMT Knype body. As the company's own body building operation was being wound down, attention turned to the hugely popular Dennis Dart. Two Reeve Burgess Pointer-bodied examples had been tried out at Newcastle garage on loan from Chester City Transport and Rossendale Transport. Obviously these made a good impression as an initial batch of 19 of the 9m version was ordered with the same Reeve Burgess bodies but with coach-style seating. The first three were for Newcastle, with the others going to the newly-acquired Crosville operation at Birkenhead. A second batch of Dennis Darts to the same specification arrived in 1993 and four of these received a modified livery with more yellow for

routes X60/260, between Hanley and Stafford.

Another purchase in 1993 was of Pennine Blue of Denton, Manchester. Pennine Blue operated mainly Greater Manchester PTE tendered services in the Tameside area, running a fleet of older Bristol REs and Leyland Atlanteans. PMT soon transferred Bristol VRTs into this fleet, repainting them at first into a two-tone blue and yellow livery, but soon switching to dark blue and yellow applied in the same style as the main fleet. This didn't last long, however, as this fleet adopted PMT's red and yellow livery when it received a batch of Dennis Darts in 1994. At the same time the 'Blue' was dropped from the fleet name. From then on it was just Pennine. Integration with the Red Rider operation at nearby Stockport soon took place, and eventually the enlarged operation moved to the former Stuarts of Hyde premises at Rothesay Garage in Dukinfield.

The final acquisition was of the bus operations of Toppings Coaches of Wavertree, Merseyside, operating as Toppline. Four Leyland Lynxes joined the fleet, operating at first with Crosville fleet names on the Toppline livery. They eventually received red and yellow livery.

Above: **The Pennine operation was transferred to First Manchester in 2001. This former PMT Olympian was repainted in February of that year and is seen in First Manchester livery two months ahead of the April transfer.**

Below: **A silver coach-seated Olympian, with Workington-built Leyland body, operating on the service between Hanley and Crewe.**

Not all vehicles received the company's red and yellow however. Apart from those in Turners' livery, two Olympians had a dark blue and yellow scheme for the Hanley - Bradwell route. A handful of Leyland Nationals had a pale blue and yellow livery for the Silverdale and Bradwell Shuttles. One of the Bristol LHs got mid blue and yellow for the K12 Coppenhall Clipper. The silver livery first used on the Olympians on the Crewe - Hanley service was introduced on Dennis Darts and Optare Deltas for the Hanley - Stafford and Keele - Leek routes. A Leyland Lynx was painted in silver for the X64 Hanley - Shrewsbury service, and several Mercedes minibuses got a light green and yellow scheme for Hospitals Link routes serving the North Staffs Royal Infirmary and City General Hospitals.

The end of PMT as an independent operator, after 7½ years, came in 1994. On 22 February it was announced that the PMT Group was to be purchased by the ever-expanding Badgerline Group. Fortunately Badgerline policy was to keep the existing liveries of companies it acquired, albeit with a large badger motif appearing behind the rear wheels

of some vehicles.

Vehicle purchases from now on would be to the Badgerline standard of Plaxton Verde-bodied Dennis Lances, Pointer-bodied Dennis Darts and Beaver-bodied Mercedes-Benz minibuses. After Northern Counties was acquired by Plaxton, a few later Lances had the Northern Counties Paladin body. Exceptions were a batch of Marshall-bodied Dennis Darts for the Pennine operation and two batches of Optare MetroRiders. The Badgerline standard Dennis Dart was the longer 9.8m variant but with cloth-covered bus seats, and subsequent deliveries were to this specification.

Now that PMT was part of a bigger group transfers of vehicles between group fleets began. Interesting arrivals were dual-door Bristol VRs from Bristol Omnibus, the first dual-door double deckers in the PMT fleet. The centre doors were not used. The first batch of five Dennis Lance/Plaxton Verde buses arrived at Burslem in 1995. The first three were in standard bus livery; the last two in the silver inter-urban scheme for the 320 Hanley - Crewe service, displacing two of the silver-liveried Olympians to

Below: **Assorted DAF buses were transferred by First from York to PMT, including this Ikarus-bodied SB220 seen in Hanley Bus Station.**

Newcastle for the X39 Alton Towers - Stoke Station shuttle. These were followed in 1996 by three Lances with Northern Counties Paladin bodywork, similar to a one-off purchased for Crosville in 1994.

The merger between Badgerline and GRT in 1995 saw the formation of FirstBus, which soon became the largest bus group in the country. At first, unlike fellow large groups Stagecoach and Arriva who had adopted a standard livery, First allowed group fleets to keep their individual liveries, but with a corporate 'f' symbol in a circle on the vehicles.

More buses were now being exchanged between fleets, and in due course PMT obtained some interesting vehicles. A one-time Eastern National Leyland Tiger with Alexander T-type bodywork arrived at Newcastle from Brewers of South Wales for a school contract that required a seat-belted vehicle. Dennis Dominators with East Lancs bodies came from Capital Citybus for the Crosville operation. Three lowheight Northern Counties-bodied Leyland Olympians arrived from Calderline, and operated for Pennine and the main fleet. The Pennine operation also received some Greater Manchester Atlanteans and an ex-Timeline Leyland Tiger. Capital Citybus sent two Duple Dominant-bodied Volvo B10M service buses, while Leyland Lynxes came from the Berks Bucks Bus Co. But

When First acquired the operations of Chester Bus in 2007 the only Chester vehicles to receive First livery were seven 1999 Marshall-bodied Darts, one of which is seen in the city's bus station.

by far the most interesting were an ex-Singapore Alexander-bodied Volvo Olympian and 10 ex-New World FirstBus tri-axle Alexander-bodied Olympians.

Further imports from Hong Kong were a batch of air-conditioned dual-door Plaxton Pointer-bodied Dennis Darts which were converted to single door before entering service. They didn't stay in the Potteries too long before moving on to other FirstGroup fleets.

The tri-axles were some of the last buses to receive the red and yellow livery, as First was now introducing a standard bus livery which would eliminate the need for repaints every time inter-company transfers took place.

The Pennine garage at Dukinfield was 37 miles from Stoke-on-Trent, but only five from First Manchester's Oldham garage, so the operation was transferred to First Manchester from April 2001. Many of the Pennine buses had received First Manchester's orange 'tomato soup' livery by February, but the three-axle Olympians went straight from PMT red and yellow to First's new corporate livery of pink, indigo and off-white. The ex PMT Olympians and Lynxes didn't last long in Greater Manchester, and a couple returned to operate in the Potteries and Crewe still in orange, but did not last long enough to receive a repaint. The first vehicles to see the new corporate colours in the Potteries were the three former silver Olympians that were moved to Newcastle for the X39 Stoke Station - Alton Towers route.

Low-floor buses were now seen as the future, and the first to enter the PMT fleet were a batch of Dennis Dart SLFs for the Crosville operation. These were the first new buses to be delivered in FirstGroup 'Barbie' livery. A batch of Wright-bodied Scanias was then delivered to Chester to operate the park-and-ride service in a special livery. The first new corporate-liveried vehicles in the Potteries were nine more Wright-bodied Scanias for the route between Kidsgrove and Meir.

Second-hand buses from sister FirstGroup companies included Dennis Darts from Manchester and Centrewest; a handful of the latter entered service in London red. On the coaching side, three Plaxton-bodied Volvo B10Ms arrived from Bee Line in full Green Line livery, mainly for longer-distance routes like the X64 Hanley - Shrewsbury and X18 Hanley - Buxton.

On the Wirral peninsula age limits on Merseyside PTE contracts saw G- and H-registered Alexander-bodied Scanias arrive from First West Yorkshire, while from First Capital came a batch of dual-door Alexander RH-bodied Volvo Olympians. Although not converted to single-door, the centre doors were not used. Also arriving at Chester were some of

Unusual transfers from First Glasgow were Dennis Darts with UVG bodies. One is seen at Bentilee.

First Capital's Optare Excels, some receiving cream and purple Lynx livery for services along the North Wales coast. Some Optare Solos also carried this livery from new. The Excels didn't last too long. With a new policy of concentrating small batches of non-standard vehicles in just one fleet, they joined similar vehicles at First Manchester. The opposite happened when all First York's DAF SB220s with Optare and Ikarus bodywork came to PMT. Some of the Optare-bodied examples ran in service in their two-tone green York livery before being repainted.

In 2002 PMT was the first of FirstGroup's subsidiaries to use the group's new national fleet numbering system, where a vehicle kept its five-figure fleet number for life, even when it was transferred to other fleets. Vehicles were numbered in blocks starting at 10000 for articulated buses, 20000 for coaches, 30000 for double deckers, 40000 for minibuses, 50000 for midibuses and 60000 for single deckers. Consequently many of PMT's vehicles started each series.

As time has gone by, the fleet has become more standardised, looking much the same as any other FirstGroup subsidiary. But there are a few odd vehicles to keep things interesting, like three ex-Glasgow Alexander-bodied Olympians, originally transferred for the X39 Stoke - Alton Towers link, and a Dennis Mini Pointer Dart that came from Springfield Coachways via First Manchester. A batch of Scania OmniCity buses came to PMT in 2005 for the 101 Hanley - Stafford route. These were the first to operate in any FirstGroup company.

An operator's licence reduction in the number of vehicles that could be used because of maintenance issues forced PMT to cut routes in 2004, allowing independents to expand into its area. D&G took over a service in Hanley, and Wardles took over some school routes. Arriva became the sole operator on the previously joint X64 service between Hanley and Shrewsbury. Further retrenchment saw the X18 Hanley to Sheffield cut back to Buxton and eventually passing to D&G. Following the run in with the Traffic Commissioner a batch of seven vehicles arrived from dealer stock in white livery, two more OmniCitys and five Wright Solar-bodied Scanias, to reduce the fleet age profile.

Chester City Council put Chester City Transport up for sale in 2007, with First doing a deal to acquire the operation, but not the majority of the vehicles. The only buses that joined First were a few Marshall-bodied Dennis Darts. Most of the remaining Chester fleet was rented back to First at peppercorn rents until they were replaced by Scanias from other group fleets.

As the number of vehicles dropped so garages closed. Burslem had gone in 2004 and in 2009 Crewe was closed as an operating base, being retained as an outstation to park vehicles.

On a brighter note, a tendering success led to PMT acquiring one of Stoke-on-Trent City Council's Cityrider-liveried Dennis Darts for a contracted service which the company won from D&G. The Dart was replaced by a new Optare Versa in 2010 – the first and, at the time of writing, the only Versa to be operated by a FirstGroup company.

By 2010 PMT had just four garages; Newcastle, Adderley Green, Chester and Birkenhead, with outstations at Cheadle and Wrexham. The two Wirral garages and Wrexham outstation passed to First Manchester in July that year, and PMT ceased to be a separate business, with the rest of its operations becoming part of First Midlands, along with Leicester, Northampton and Wyvern (the one-time Midland Red West company).

So in the last 30 years PMT has been part of NBC, then an independent company which consolidated its position in its home area by buying up its competitors. It has expanded into new territory, only to be purchased by a bigger group and then reduced in size as parts were hived off to other group companies. Issues with maintenance have allowed competitors to get a foothold and subsequently expand in what was PMT's core operating area.

One can only wonder what might have been if the company has stayed independent.

www.firstgroup.com

The only Optare Versa operated by First is this bus owned by Stoke-on-Trent City Council and run under contract by PMT on a Cityrider service between Tunstall and Middleport.

Tayside's Ailsa fleet totalled 161 vehicles at its peak, most of which had two-door Alexander bodies. A 1979 example is seen in Dundee High Street in May 1994. Many of these buses had their centre exits removed; this one retains its original two-door layout.

Dundee
delights

BILLY NICOL illustrates the Tayside Transport fleet in the mid-1990s, showing the vehicles in operation prior to the purchase of the employee-owned company by National Express in 1997.

Ten Northern Counties-bodied Mark III Ailsas joined the Tayside fleet in 1983. All of Tayside's Mark III Ailsas were long – 10.3m – models. These were the only new Northern Counties-bodied Ailsas for a Scottish fleet.

In 1983 Tayside took 25 Ailsas with East Lancs bodies, a combination unique to the Tayside fleet. This bus is seen in Dundee in 1995.

Tayside switched from front-engined Ailsas to mid-engined Citybuses, taking two batches totalling 20. The last 15 were delivered in 1989 and had Alexander R-type bodies. This is a 1996 view, with the Citybus in the recently-introduced Tayside Buses livery. These were the last new double-deckers for the fleet for 15 years.

Minibuses played a very small part in Tayside's operations. Four Dodge S56s with 23-seat Alexander AM-type bodies, a combination more commonly seen with Scottish Bus Group companies, joined the Tayside fleet in 1987. This is a 1995 view.

The last small buses for Tayside before the business was sold to National Express were three Optare MetroRider 29-seaters delivered in 1996.

In 1993 several single-deckers were purchased by Tayside for evaluation, including four East Lancs-bodied Scania N113CRBs. These were of step-entrance layout, and were followed by a solitary N113CRL, also bodied by East Lancs, which was Scotland's first new-generation low-entry bus.

Above: **Another 1993 purchase by Tayside was this ex-demonstration Volvo B10B with Northern Counties Paladin body, acquired when just a few months old. It was a 49-seater.**

Below: **The Volvo was not Tayside's only ex-demonstrator. This bus, new in 1992, was one of the original Dennis Lance demonstrators and had a 47-seat Plaxton Verde body. It was one of two ex-demonstration Lances in the fleet. The other had a Northern Counties body, generally similar to that on the B10B illustrated above.**

The Damory story

MICHAEL H. C. BAKER looks back at the development of a small Dorset business which is now part of the Go-Ahead group.

"Don't forget to take some trinkets for the natives, coloured beads go down well," was the advice from a friend when I mentioned I was venturing out of Purbeck up to the far north of Dorset into the area served by Damory Coaches of Blandford. It's probably more a reflection on us than on them, but there is a perception that that part of county, away from the sea and without the many incomers, is a world apart. And it is true that with its deep valleys, high hills, ancient but small towns, villages and hamlets it is almost a caricature of the ancient, unchanging rural England perceived by sentimental strangers.

An unusual Ikarus-bodied DAF SB220, seen in Bournemouth in 1995. It had been new in 1994 to Manchester operator Walls, hence the WAL

Blandford Forum (note the Roman origins of its name) may not register on the national scale as one of the nation's significant transport hubs, yet the story of the public transport which has served it and its deeply rural hinterland in the last 50 years or so is vastly more complex and a good deal more fascinating than one might suppose. A handsome, largely Georgian town following a fire in 1731, Blandford's population is around 9,000, swelled slightly by the big army camp out on the Salisbury road and the some 600-plus boys and girls of Bryanston public school set in extensive grounds beside the River Stour, which forms the western boundary of the town. There was once a railway at Blandford, the Somerset & Dorset, which closed in 1966, the popularity of which seems to grow in inverse proportion to the number of people who actually travelled on it, few trains other than holiday specials seeming to have ever carried more than three men and a dog, possibly accompanied by the odd pig and sheep, as they wound their leisurely way through the undulating, under-

A Wilts & Dorset Bristol VRT crests North Street in Wareham on the service to Swanage.

The name Damory derives from a local, ancient, enormous, hollow oak tree which in Cromwell's time measured 68ft in circumference with room inside for 20 men. When the Great Fire of Blandford occurred in 1731 two families, who had been made homeless by the fire, lived in the tree for a time. Sadly, 24 years later it was felled and sold for firewood, but it gave its name to a local pub, and, of course, to the bus and coach company.

Having established his business credentials, Vic's operation flourished. To settle a debt, he took as payment a school contract with a vehicle. So it was that Damory was born as an operator in the early 1970s. Slowly the fleet developed, operating school contracts and private hire with a variety of Bedfords, Transits and Sherpas. It became obvious that the Damory coach operation was outgrowing its base so Vic, his family and his staff built the garage at the bottom of Tin Pot Lane which still forms the coach and administration centre for the operation.

Following a request from local residents at Pimperne, just outside Blandford, a stage carriage service was added, one day a week, with one journey in each direction. The operation settled into a steady, well-respected, business. It did not really feature on the Wilts & Dorset radar.

By the 1980s Vic recognized that he had two options – to invest heavily in the fleet or to sell. The fleet at that time comprised six coaches (five Bedfords and one Seddon), six Transits and two Sherpas. His son and daughter, whilst they

populated countryside between Bath and Poole and Bournemouth.

Wilts & Dorset was always the premier player in connecting Blandford with the outside world, with a garage, and services to Weymouth and Dorchester, Wimborne, Poole, Bournemouth, Shaftesbury and Salisbury. Wilts & Dorset hasn't gone, although its garage has, but Damory, which is part, as we shall see, of the Wilts & Dorset empire, has been an increasing presence in Blandford Forum since the early 1970s.

Strange as it may seem, the company's history starts near Winchester. The founder of Damory Coaches, Vic Kimber, was born in North Waltham and went to school at Dummer. On leaving school Vic joined Sparsholt College in Winchester as a mechanic, a very practical trade which would come in useful. Vic wished to spread his wings. On seeing an advert for the Damory filling station in Blandford he decided to take the plunge, and moved his family to the town in November 1969 to operate the filling station and garage.

Three former Wilts and Dorset VRs in the Damory fleet, at Poole in 1999.

A former City of Oxford Volvo B10B with Plaxton Verde body, new in 1995 and acquired by Damory ten years later.

participated in the business, were not interested in taking it over. Vic was in his mid-50s: should he sleep easy at night, or invest heavily? With an eye to local circumstances he decided to sell and sleep at night. This was the first of a number of such sales throughout the area.

Wilts & Dorset at that time – 1992/93 – was five years into privatization and entering a more stable operating environment. It had seen off Badgerline operations in Poole and Salisbury, but only at considerable cost. It took Wilts & Dorset a long time to recover financially.

And changes were afoot in the unlikely setting of Blandford Forum. Oakfield Travel, an operator in Blandford, and the Stanbridge & Crichel Bus Company, a long-established business, had merged in 1989. In the early 1990s the owners wished to retire, so the company was sold to British Bus, through its subsidiary Guildford & West Surrey. The new owners launched themselves into expansion mode by obtaining work with under-priced tenders.

Now we move back 20 years in order to meet Ian Gray who knows more about Damory than anyone living. It was on 1 July 1973 that he started work at

the Square, Bournemouth, with Hants & Dorset, a name that was to rise and fall. Ian joined the traffic department straight from school – except that they didn't know he was starting! One of his new colleagues was Mike Power who was planning the absorption of the King Alfred services in Winchester into the Hants & Dorset network. Eventually Andrew Bryce, who worked in the same office, noticed, in Ian's own words, "that I could write, so our long working relationship started". Andrew was planning many changes – Hants & Dorset was, for instance, still operating to Beech House which had been a World War II refugee camp – and Ian, as schedules clerk, had ten enjoyable years, during which as a local management trainee he undertook most tasks found in a bus company. With privatization looming and the break up of Hants & Dorset, everyone had to apply for new jobs with Wilts & Dorset in 1983. Ian became operating supervisor at Poole depot and eventually assistant district manager.

One day, some ten years later, Ian received a call from Andrew Bryce. He was expecting to discuss a new vehicle defect system but instead was asked if he'd like to move to Damory, which was being taken over by Wilts & Dorset, and manage it. After some thought Ian agreed and off he went to the far north – well, to Blandford. To prevent others from using the Hants & Dorset name it was decided that Damory would be the trading name of Hants & Dorset Motor Services. Once again Ian was an employee of Hants & Dorset, albeit a different company from the original. May is not an ideal time to join a coach business as the season is fast picking up. After the initial handover Ian was left on his own to run the business, just about everything from making up wage packets to detailing staff. And when push came to shove he would have to drive.

Other acquisitions followed and in 1993 Oakfield Travel and Stanbridge & Crichel passed to Wilts & Dorset/Damory, and this take-over included premises at Sunrise Business Park, Blandford and at Stanbridge. Staff also passed into Ian's care and also, in Ian's own words, "a rag bag of vehicles," most of them elderly and not very reliable. Many of these were parked at the Stanbridge garage, deemed unfit for service, and were replaced by a shadow fleet of white vehicles. For a time Andrew Bryce was also

The preserved Wilts & Dorset Bristol VR in the Damory depot, Blandford, in November, 2010. The bus was new in 1979.

based in Blandford, the centre of operations, and he set a policy of dropping the names of Oakfield and Stanford & Crichel, and abandoning Stanbridge garage with its difficult access and poor facilities.

Having control over the routes and school services over a wide area allowed Andrew Bryce to recast the network. This took much of the winter and allowed Ian to deal with the day-to-day problems and improve reliability. The recasting included absorbing the business of the Blandford Bus Company, following a period of competition with Wilts & Dorset. In the spring of 1994 the new network was introduced. The opportunity was taken to inter-work movements and combine school runs. This saw the introduction of the first of a long line of Bristol VRs and a proper standard timetable. VRs lasted well into the 21st century with Wilts & Dorset and even longer with Damory; a Wilts & Dorset preserved example is still based at the Damory depot and occasionally fills in on school runs. During this time much work was undertaken with Dorset County Council to establish a firm financial basis for the network. A good partnership was forged and all involved could see the benefits that strong local ownership and management brought.

By the end of the 1990s Damory operations had settled into a reasonable pattern of workings with between 40 and 45 vehicles and a reliable and largely well-established workforce. Damory vehicles have largely been cascaded from the main Wilts & Dorset fleet; quite often examples of types no longer in Wilts & Dorset colours can still be sampled in Damory service, although it is also possible to find both fleets operating identical types.

Many of Damory's routes are intensely rural. Market day has always provided good business, with the biggest and most popular town in the company's catchment area being Salisbury. Salisbury is not large by city standards. It retains much of the air of a market town set in the countryside, and it is still possible to walk along the water meadows with sheep on either side, take in that incomparable view of the cathedral framed by trees immortalized by Constable, and be in the city centre within seven minutes.

One morning last summer I caught the company's Tuesdays-only 314 service outside Blandford Hospital. The 314 consists of just one journey out and back from Broadstone to Salisbury. The direct route to Salisbury, worked by Wilts & Dorset, takes a different route out of the town, circumnavigates the army camp (where a sentry comes aboard and

In 2011 Damory expanded rapidly. An Optare Solo is seen in Blandford Forum on the service to Yeovil. The route operates three round trips on weekdays, two on Saturdays.

Damory branding on a Wilts & Dorset Olympian in Poole in September 2011. The Leyland-bodied bus had been new to Southern Vectis.

A DAF DB250 with Optare Spectra body pauses in Affpuddle on the infrequent cross-country service from Poole to Dorchester in November 2010.

checks upstairs and down), and then heads straight along the A354, but the 314 is specifically scheduled to serve as many villages and hamlets as possible and in doing so negotiates some lanes so narrow I'd be wary of driving anything much wider than a wheelbarrow along them, the hedgerows brushing the bus windows on both sides simultaneously.

Although almost empty when I boarded, whoever had devised the schedule, quite possibly Ian himself, had done his work well for we picked up passengers all the way, the route taking us half way to Shaftesbury before turning east at Fontmell Magna, calling at the appropriately named Hill Farm (Crossroads), then Tarrant Gunville (village hall), followed by Tarrant Hinton (Council Houses), before

joining the main A354 at Tarrant Hinton (Gunville Turn) 49 minutes after leaving Blandford but only four miles from it as the crow flies. From here on the driver was able to put his foot down and with no takers at either Gussage St. Michael or Gussage St. Andrews and ignoring Gussage All Saints entirely, we sped down the main road and needed only a further 31 minutes to reach Salisbury.

In the summer of 2003 the Wilts & Dorset Group was sold to Go-Ahead, following the desire of some of the directors to retire. Go-Ahead pursues what many think is the excellent policy of allowing its companies to retain their individual liveries, and Ray Stenning's Best Impressions studio has devised a very attractive livery for Damory. Vehicles continue to be cascaded from both Wilts & Dorset and sister Go-Ahead company Southern Vectis, as well as being acquired from other sources.

From September, 2011, Damory vehicles could be seen as far north as Yeovil in Somerset, as far east as Brockenhurst in Hampshire and within sight of the Devon border at Lyme Regis. This was as a result of being awarded many more school and college contracts. Many more vehicles had to be acquired, mainly Optare Solos, along with many more drivers. This all went less than smoothly, creating much media attention, but that part of the story must be told some other time...

www.southerncoachhire.co.uk

A Leyland-bodied Olympian illustrates the deep rural nature of Damory's operating area. It is seen in Bloxworth.

This Dennis Trident was new to Metrobus of Crawley in 1999 and joined the Network Colchester fleet in 2007. Its East Lancs body was originally of two-door layout for operation in London. It was rebuilt as a single-door bus for operation in Colchester and upseated from 69 to 72. It carries branding for cross-town service 8.

Network Colchester

It is 20 years since municipal bus operation ended in Colchester. The spiritual successor to Colchester Borough Transport is Network Colchester, part of the TGM group, and operator of the town's local bus services since 2004. **GEOFF MILLS** illustrates a selection of the buses which have been operated by the company.

With the town's castle in the background, a Dennis Dart SLF with unusual Caetano Compass body turns into Queen Street in the summer of 2008. It was new in 2001 to TGM, and was one of six operated by Network Colchester.

Among many second-hand double-deckers operated by Network Colchester is this Northern Counties-bodied Scania N113 which started life in 1990 with Liverline of Liverpool. It joined Network Colchester in 2008.

Above: Another second-hand N113 is this bus which had been new to Derby City Transport in 1995 and arrived in Colchester in 2009 by way of Arriva Derby. In the absence of route branding the wording on the side of the East Lancs body proclaims that the bus is 'Serving the local community'. Arriva Derby was indirectly associated with Network Colchester following the purchase of TGM by Arriva in 2008.

Left: There have been new Scanias too, with six new double-deckers being purchased between 2005 and 2009. This is a 2008 N230UD loading in the High Street. It has a 79-seat East Lancs Olympus body.

A number of buses from other TGM companies have operated for short periods in Colchester. This DAF DB250 was new to another Essex operator, Harris Bus, in 1998, and is seen arriving in Colchester on the service from Ipswich via East Bergholt in May 2008. It has a Northern Counties Palatine II body and is in the livery of Wiltax of New Haw, a business which had been acquired by TGM the previous month.

Two long-wheelbase Dennis Tridents with 82-seat Alexander ALX400 bodies were acquired from Arriva Northumbria in 2009. They were new in 2000.

A rather different 2009 acquisition was this high-floor Volvo Citybus, which was 20 years old when it took to the streets of Colchester. It had been new to London Country South West, and has a Northern Counties 84-seat body.

Also new to London Country South West in 1989 is this Citybus with East Lancs body, seen in Queen Street in 2010 followed by two Plaxton-bodied Dennis Darts.

There have been single-deck Volvos too, such as this B10BLE with Alexander ALX300 body, photographed in Monkwick Estate in 2010. It had been new to TGM in 2000 for operation on the former Green Line 726 service between Heathrow and Bromley.

A 2011 addition to the fleet was this five-year-old Dennis Dart SLF with 29-seat Plaxton Pointer body. Its previous ownership – Tellings Golden Miller – is displayed above the door. The orange beacon on the roof shows that it was used at Heathrow airport.

Another bus with a Heathrow connection is this air-conditioned Scania OmniCity, one of six purchased in 2011 from Menzies, which had provided contracted services at the airport. They were bought for operation on an hourly service between the University of Essex and Stansted Airport. This bus is seen in Braintree in July 2011, in its first week of operation. These Scanias have just 36 seats, and additional luggage racks.

Jones Login

five decades in south-west Wales

LES DICKINSON tells the story of one of the best-known coach operators in south-west Wales.

All photographs by the author.

Today the man at the helm of the company which trades simply as Jones Login, is Endaf Jones, whose father Arwel started the business in 1965. Yet you have to go back even further to understand how the business really began. Idwal Jones, grandfather of Endaf, joined forces with Clodwyn Thomas, to form a business known as Thomas & Jones Clunderwen Ltd in 1945. Clunderwen is a village in Pembrokeshire sitting astride the A478 some 14 miles north of the popular holiday resort of Tenby.

The company later became Precelly Motors, taking its name from the Preseli Hills, or Mynydd Preseli, which form part of the Pembrokeshire Coast National Park.

During the first 20 years of operation the business ran assorted Bedfords and Leylands, the latter including an ex-Southdown Tiger PS1 with Windover bodywork, and an ex-Western Welsh Royal Tiger bus. In common with many other operators in west and south Wales, the company became a regular buyer of former Western Welsh vehicles.

The changes in the mid 1960s followed the death of Idwal Jones in 1964. That's when his son Arwel formed what we now know as Jones Login.

In December 1967, Arwel bought the first new coach for the business, a Bedford VAL70, which cost £5,500. Other VALs followed, including one with rare Weymann Topaz bodywork. Other additions to

Top: **Most new coaches purchased by Jones Login in recent years have had Plaxton bodies, as illustrated by a Volvo B10M outside the company's modern workshop.**

Left: **The purchase of new buses by Jones Login is rare. The most recent is this compact 2009 Optare Solo M710SE. It is a 19-seater and is seen on the service between Login and Carmarthen, which operates only on Wednesdays and Saturdays.**

the fleet in the 1960s and 1970s included Leyland Tiger Cubs from Western Welsh, various Bedfords, and even a couple of Bristol LLs. There were new coaches too, including two Bedford YRTs with smart Plaxton Elite Express III coachwork, purchased in 1973 and 1974 respectively.

The company broadened its horizons in 1976 with its first Continental tour; Ostend was the destination.

The current large and well-equipped garage was built in 1977 with a modern purpose-built office added in 1986. A large outdoor parking lot lies directly opposite the depot. During the average day this lot is far from full as many of the vehicles used on school contracts remain at, or near, the schools which they are serving. Jones Login runs 11 school contracts at the time of writing.

Expansion came in December 1980 when Jones acquired the fleet and licences of Pioneer of Laugharne. Some interesting vehicles came with this take-over, including two former Midland Red Ford R192s with Plaxton bus bodies.

New Bedfords continued to arrive, and while most were full-size coaches they were joined in 1982 by four Bedford CF 12-seaters. These were useful both as feeders for the company's excursions, or for use on school contracts to and from the many small isolated villages served by the business. When Bedford stopped making coaches Jones Login, like many other family-run coach business, switched to the Dennis Javelin.

Changing travel patterns saw the arrival in 1987 of the first coach to be fitted with a toilet and

There have also been Plaxton-bodied Dennises. This Javelin has a 53-seat Profile body and was new in 2007.

This Irizar-bodied Scania K94 is unusual in having 70 seats and is used mainly on school work, as seen here outside Crymych primary school.

reclining seats. It was a Duple-bodied Volvo B10M. In 2001 it received a dual purpose body by East Lancs to extend its life.

A new look was adopted in 1992, inspired by the livery on a demonstration coach. Its livery style was adopted with the Jones Login colour scheme of turquoise, white and midnight blue. The coach that was first to be presented in this way was a Volvo B10M with Plaxton Premiere 350 coachwork. In 1999 Jones Login achieved the coveted CoachMarque quality standard awarded by the Confederation of Passenger Transport. To achieve CoachMarque many areas of the business come under scrutiny including the specification, standards and rigorous routine maintenance procedure for vehicles, approved staff training policy, driver standards including smart uniform, and passenger care.

There is a regular infusion of high-specification rolling stock into this fleet. For example, the 2010 addition was a Volvo B9R with Plaxton's new Elite body, at a cost of around £220,000 – a far cry from that first new coach that Arwel Jones bought for £5,500 in 1967.

The village of Login is actually reached by a labyrinth of small roads and country lanes from Clunderwen. First sighting of the garage leaves visitors wondering how the larger vehicles of today gain access to it via these restricted roads.

All 25 members of the Jones Login team can be called upon to drive if required and the Jones family are justifiably proud of their dedicated workforce. The company is also dedicated – to the development of all staff to CoachMarque standards.

And it shows.

This Volvo B10M started life as a Duple-bodied coach, bought new in 1987. It was fitted with this 70-seat East Lancs body in 2001. The location is Carmarthen bus park, where it is laying over after working the Wednesdays-only service from Glandwr.

An enthusiast's A to Z

PETER ROWLANDS offers an idiosyncratic list of landmarks in his 30 years of bus photography

All photographs by the author.

A

Arrival: the agony of not knowing where to go to get the best bus photographs, or how best to make use of limited time. Where do the buses hang out?

A could be for Arriva, but I still can't somehow forgive Arriva for obliterating the identities of all those bus companies it ended up owning.

A is also for Alexander – once the biggest bus operator in Scotland, and still the name of Britain's foremost bus bodybuilder (if you append 'Dennis', that is).

A for Atlantean, or B for Blackpool? This bus started out in 1972 as an Alexander-bodied double-decker with Bradford Corporation, but later gained this Northern Counties single-deck bodywork. It is seen in 1998.

B for Badgerline and Y for yellow – A Bristol RE in post-National Bus livery in 1989.

A is for Ailsa, Volvo's answer back in the 1970s to all those requests for a bus "like they used to make them", notably with the engine at the front. But with their cramped cab and awkward access, they weren't really the solution Volvo wanted them to be.

And A is for Atlantean – the vehicle that arguably defined the double-decker bus for a whole generation.

B

B could stand for bendibus, but I'm in two minds about that. Too long for our cramped streets, too austere in their limited seating, too draughty in winter (all those doors). Or do you like them? B is certainly for Blackpool, with its long-lasting open-platform Leyland Titans and its balloon trams.

Maybe B is just for bodywork. How old were you when you finally came to comprehend that 'make' of a bus meant the largely hidden chassis or underframe, not what you could actually see?

No, B is for Bristol. The manufacturer, I mean, not the city. With their standard liveries and ECW bodies, Bristol buses sometimes seemed almost invisible; but they were a subliminal reminder that someone else made buses too.

C

Coaches are buses by association, really. I'll photograph them if they're rather unusual, or maybe if they belong to the local bus company. But do they really count?

And what if it's a coach with bus seats, or conversely a bus pretending to be a coach? Remember how we used to get hung up over the difference between a bus and a semi-coach? Maybe the Americans have got it right; they don't discriminate – they simply call them all busses.

Maybe C should stand for council-run fleets instead. Forty years ago they were the norm, and company-run buses were the oddities, often running on country and suburban routes. How things change.

D

Daimler never sounded like a name for a bus maker. No wonder people who didn't know thought Daimler buses must be extra-luxurious. I wish.

The same thing still happens. A lot of passengers think a Mercedes-Benz bus must by definition be posher than a Dennis. Maybe D stands for 'don't know any better'.

Anyway, Dennis has the Ds. Dennis is the survivor that jumped in when Leyland was floundering in the 1970s. Leyland had gained a virtual monopoly of UK bus manufacture (owning AEC, Bristol and Daimler by then), and the market wasn't having it. Dennis was its secret weapon

– and it all worked out rather well. Leyland is long gone, but Alexander Dennis is still with us.

E

E is for the enticing, energising power of the chase, and the ecstasy of success; but there isn't enough of all this around. You think you've got the best bus picture of your life; then it turns out you were suffering from camera shake, or the bus had an incomplete destination display and a massive scrape along the lower panel.

With Photoshop you can repair a lot of these blemishes nowadays, but it's not quite the same thing as getting it right first time.

Actually E is for Eastern Coach Works; and no, I'm not obsessed with Bristol and ECW. But it's easy to forget how significant this bodybuilder once was. I remember the managing director once telling me his factory was turning out 500 bodies a year. If only.

F

F is for Fleetline (see D for Daimler). Fleetlines were the greener grass on the other

F for First. Where would we be without this cheery colour scheme? This is a long-wheelbase Dennis Dart SLF with Plaxton Pointer bodywork, seen in Portsmouth in 1998.

side of the fence: rear-engined buses powered by the legendary Gardner engine, instead of the Leyland units of equivalent Atlanteans. But they suffered driveline problems over the years too, and London disposed of its big fleet prematurely.

You could argue that F is for front engine, which for decades was what the industry thought buses should have (see A for Ailsa). But I'm not one to push water uphill.

Which is why F must be for First. I don't like the ubiquity of the 'Barbie' bus livery any more than that of Arriva's, but intrinsically I find it rather cheering.

I for independent: here, Green Bus Service, which was running this Roe-bodied ex West Yorkshire PTE Atlantean in 1996. It is seen in Wolverhampton.

G

Glasgow – scene of 1980s bus wars; the progenitor of a livery that percolated through to Halifax, then to Aberdare, and still pops up to this day; home to Albion double- and single-deckers. A

G for Go Ahead, A for Atlantean. Seen in Darlington in 1992, this bus sums up the way NBC subsidiaries cautiously departed from the corporate look.

good place to photograph buses.

Yet I find myself drawn to Guy. It was never numero uno in the bus world, but it was definitely a player, and there were still hundreds of Guys around in the 1970s, when I started taking a real interest.

Actually, though, G is for Go Ahead, simply because it gets the full marks in the Campaign for Real Bus Liveries. Not all of them pass muster; but in places like Brighton and Hove you find an operator that truly understands the point of local identity, and the value of history.

Go Go Ahead.

H

H is for horizontal underfloor engines, which were prevalent in heavyweight single-deckers from the 1950s onwards. The AEC Reliance and Leyland Leopard (then Tiger) defined buses of their kind for a generation. With today's array of different engine positions

and locations, that's hard now to imagine.

H could be for Halifax (no, we've been there) or Huddersfield. But actually I think it's for Hull, where traces of pre-war streamlining persisted in the council's bus bodies built right up the 1960s, and East Yorkshire bought those extraordinary chamfered-roof double-decker to slide under Beverley Bar.

I

Have you tried approaching BMW or Nissan lately and asking for the rear light cluster on your next car to be put in a slightly different position from your next-door neighbour's? I don't think you'd have a lot of success with that.

Yet over the years, bus fleet engineers have done exactly this with their suppliers – and got away with it. And makers have sometimes encouraged them, coming up with vehicles they didn't even know they wanted.

So I is for idiosyncratic, whether it's Nottingham's peculiar front and rear ends, or Manchester's glorious deep-screened Mancunians, or something rather stranger (the Gnu? the Knype?).

Or does I stand for independents – operators who often hang on the periphery of the industry, but whose indomitable enthusiasm helps sustain it?

J

J is for Javelin – a modest underfloor-engined bus and coach chassis that underlined Dennis's return to the passenger vehicle market – and which, amazingly, was in the company's catalogue for 25 years.

Or is J for joint operations? They were common once (Newcastle Corporation/ Gateshead & District, Halifax, Brighton Corporation/Brighton Hove & District). Nowadays, operators who seek to work together risk being accused of price fixing or collusion – unless of course the local authority orchestrates it.

No; I know what J stands for. It's Jesmond, that trendy inner suburb of Newcastle, where flat-shares jostle with elegant Victorian houses converted into hotels, and yellow trolleybuses once turned on their shortest route.

K

K is for K-type. Yes, we're back with Bristol double-deckers, and specifically the maker's post-war double-deck range. Along with

J is for Jesmond, S is for Scania and Y is for Tyne & Wear's yellow livery. This distinctive Alexander PS-bodied N113 is seen on Osborne Road in 1998.

London's RTs, and perhaps the Leyland Titan with the company's own Farington body design, Ks and later KSWs helped define for a generation what a bus was supposed to look like. Square but elegantly curved at the corners, they oozed dependability.

Or maybe K is for Keighley – an example of a place whose identity seems to wax and wane

according to whether the buses have local branding or not. After the anonymous PTE/NBC era, Blazefield's 'Keighley & District' branding gave the place new definition.

L

L is for Leyland. Even before British Leyland was born in the 1960s, Leyland had emerged as the UK's largest bus and truck builder. But in fact it had simply grown too big for its own good, and 20 years later was gone.

L is also for London, whose immense buying strength dominated the bus industry for decades, and whose unique route tendering policy has ensured that it still stands apart from other bus operators, with a more or less standardised colour scheme and uniform fares.

And L is for lowbridge –

K is for Knype, a rather formless body built by operator PMT itself, and based here on the short-lived Leyland Swift midibus chassis. Seen in the Potteries in 1998.

Top left: **L is for Leyland – of course. This striking Olympian in the Armchair fleet is seen in Ealing in 1996.** Top right: **M is for MCW, and also for Metrobus. This Mk I model, seen in service with Capital Citybus in Chingford in 1992, was new to South Yorkshire PTE eleven years before.**

double-deckers built up to the 1960s with a low roof and four-abreast upper-deck seating with a sunken side gangway. Hateful things. And for Lodekka, which beat the problem with a drop-centre back axle that lowered everything; and the similar Loline from Dennis and Lowlander from Albion.

M

Metro-Cammell Weymann once seemed like the new future of the bus industry – transforming itself (as Optare and Wright have done

more recently) from bodybuilder to complete bus manufacturer. Once in the late 1980s there was even the prospect that it would merge with Leyland and dominate the UK bus industry. But it never happened, and instead MCW's owner, the Laird group, simply lost heart and sold off the business in bits. M is for Might Have Been.

Or maybe M is for minibuses, a feature of the new dawn that flickered with bus deregulation in the 1980s, then faded away. No, M is for Midland Red, the company that for so long dared to do what even London shied away from: build its own buses.

N

The National Bus Company was a bit like Arriva and First and Stagecoach all rolled into one, but without their entrenched presence in the major metropolitan centres. If you grew up in the NBC years, you probably miss its uniform green or red liveries and standardised fleetnames. If you knew all the individual brands and liveries that it ousted in the early 1970s, you may well have hated it with equal fervency.

Or maybe N is for Leyland National, a curious Government-inspired concoction set up by Leyland and National Bus in the early 1970s. This single-decker

N is for National, the bus so many of us loved to hate for ousting Bristol REs from production – but one that proved surprisingly durable. This United Counties example, originally green, had acquired a red Aylesbury livery by 1986.

range ousted many other models that some people preferred – notably the Bristol RE.

And N is for Northern General – one of the few large operators which, like Midland Red, called the shots on their own bus designs in the inter-war years and after.

O

Open-top buses: do they count? I'm in two minds. I photograph them if there's nothing else to get excited about, but I do it with misgivings. They seem slightly fake.

I could say O was for open platform, which survived sixty or so years of motor bus operation (a hundred if you count Routemaster operation). But Borismaster or not, we've moved on.

O is also for Olympian, the British standard double-decker between 1980 and 2000. Once seemingly permanent; now fast disappearing.

No, O is for Optare, which means hope, and is what its owners have clung to since its creation nearly 30 years ago from Charles H Roe, one of Leyland's

bodybuilding operations. Thanks to the recent intervention of Ashok Leyland in India, it's still with us.

P

P is for Plaxton – of course. Established more than 100 years ago, Plaxton is one of the truly enduring brands in the UK bus industry. And yes, it *does* count as a bus builder, having developed the massively successful Pointer body for the Dennis Dart, then its Enviro200 successor. And after the group acquired Northern Counties in 1995, the Plaxton name even appeared on mainstream double-deckers.

P also stands for preserved buses. I always promise myself I won't take too many photographs of them (a poor substitute for catching them in the wild), but I always do anyway.

Actually P is for Putney, just because I live there, and because of its marvellous confluence of bus routes.

Q is for Q-type, P for preserved – but there's surprisingly little in this view on Brighton sea front to reveal that it was taken in the 1990s.

Q

Q could be for "quest". Written with a small q, it's what drives us whenever we go out with a camera.

Written with an initial capital, Q could stand for Quest 80 – a short-lived and little-remembered

chassis manufacturer based in Telford, which produced a few rear-engined coaches in the mid-1980s, primarily for Excelsior of Bournemouth.

But I think Q stands for Q-type – a remarkably modern-looking bus built by AEC in the early 1930s, with a full front and an engine mounted vertically on the offside. Most were withdrawn

prematurely, but it gave an early flavour of how all buses would look from the 1960s onwards.

R

Don't look so surprised. Did you think R would stand for anything else? The Routemaster wasn't the first front-engined, rear-entrance bus; in fact it was more or less the last, both to be made and to be operated in large numbers. But it came to sum up this traditional type of vehicle. It's the living embodiment of the over-used term 'iconic'.

S is for Stagecoach, whose original livery looks unfamiliar on this 1993 Cambus Marshall-bodied Dennis Dart, seen in Cambridge five years later.

Mind you, R also stands for Regent. In the day, a lot of us thought that was the definitive double-decker bus – especially London's RT version. Then there was the Renown – a sort of cross between a Bridgemaster and a Regent. I also had a soft spot for the Reliance single-decker. Oh, and what about its predecessor, the Regal?

There's no easy way to tell you this: R stands for AEC.

S

S is for Stagecoach, and for the stupendous drive of Brian Souter, the man behind it. It's another corporate that denied us variety in bus liveries, but it's given us a lot in return: stability, strength, and support for British bus building.

S is also for Scania – ever the also-ran in the double-deck market, but exhibiting extraordinary staying power, and now better established than ever.

S is for Standards – that is, standard double-deck bodies, 1970s Manchester-style. In a world of idiosyncrasy, it suited bodybuilders to have a basic design to fall back on, and if you include London's rather more square-cut Daimlers, derivatives could eventually be found up and down the land.

T

T is for Trident. If the Dominator and Javelin were statements of intent, the Trident was the confirmation. It said Dennis really and truly was a serious contender in the bus market, and wasn't

T is for Titan, and this is one of the small batch of 15 built for Greater Manchester at the end of the 1970s. It is seen in 1986.

going away.

T is also for trainers – terrifying for the would-be bus drivers who have to contend with them; simultaneously trying not to look like a bus at all, and grasping for some elusive identity that its current operator never had.

And T is for Tyne & Wear – not just because that's where I come from, but also because it's always given us such a profusion of bus companies, model types and colour schemes.

U

U is for United Automobile Services. It's long gone now, but those of us with long memories can't help but marvel at a company whose territory once stretched from Northumberland right down past the Wash. After it was split up, components like United (North East) and Eastern

Counties (East Anglia) continued to share a common identity.

U is for underfloor engines, but we've been there already. Save a thought, though, for the double-decker variety – notably Volvo's step-entrance CityBus: yet another ill-judged bid by the company to provide what it thought operators wanted. Maybe U is just for urban transport, which is what all this is mostly about.

V

Volvo succeeded where most other foreign manufacturers have failed; it became a market leader in Britain's mainstream passenger vehicle market – first in coaches, then (with its Leyland acquisition) in double-decker buses. It almost feels like a local manufacturer now, even though it builds its buses elsewhere.

But V stands for vertical

engines, too – both transverse, as found in most modern double-deckers, and longitudinal, as in relatively rare models such as the Bristol VRL.

And V also stands for V engine – something even rarer in the bus world, in Britain at least. Dennis tried Mercedes-Benz units in its limited-run Falcon V, of which only eight double-deck versions were built.

W

W is West Midlands, I suppose: first the passenger transport executive, then its successor, West Midlands Travel. I never quite got the idea of that name, though; 'travel' sounds like something you do over long distances, not across town.

Anyway, its constituent municipal operations often supported local bus builders (Guy in Wolverhampton, Daimler in Coventry, then later MCW in Birmingham); so all credit there.

Actually, though, W is for Willowbrook. Such a nice name for a bodybuilder; such a shame it

ended up with a poor reputation for quality and style. W is for what might have been.

X

X is for XA Atlanteans, of which London Transport bought 50 in 1985 to gain its first experience of rear-engined buses. After a few years they were sold on (mostly to Hong Kong), and I never saw a single one, so I can't say they have much resonance for me personally. I wish I had though. Their Park Royal bodywork was not unlike the MCW bodies I knew from Newcastle, so they would have seemed quite familiar.

Y

Y is yellow buses. I've never seen any that don't look bright and cheery. In my home town of Newcastle they were the norm; and look how well yellow worked with Alexander Northern, Bournemouth and Clydeside, with its arresting yellow and red.

And think of the dramatic and unforgettable yellow, red and blue livery of Bristol CityBus: that wonderful flowering of local identity back in the 1980s, when the shackles of NBC were finally shaken off.

You can probably think of others, such as Badgerline, Stevensons of Uttoxeter, Midland Red West and Mainline in Sheffield. Yellow gets splashed about every time operators remember that buses should be *fun*. There can never be enough of that.

Z

Z is zeal, and if you think that's a cop-out, I agree. But you tell me what else Z stands for. Zeal is certainly what a lot of us have shown over the years, sometimes going to unbelievable lengths for the photo we felt we must have. Or maybe it's just for Zen, which could mean a lot of things, but in this context probably just means being grateful: for the operators, the vehicles, the enthusiasm, the time to pursue it and the pleasure it's brought over the years.

Captivated by Switzerland

There's more to Switzerland than mountains, watches and cuckoo clocks. **TONY GREAVES** shares his fascination with the country's Post buses.

My first visit to Switzerland was as a fifth-former on a school trip to Interlaken in 1967. From the first sighting of a normal-control Saurer I was hooked. This was no Bedford OB, but a full-size bus, in a superb Newcastle-like cadmium yellow and silver livery with a huge chrome radiator grille surround at the front of a very long bonnet.

From that first sighting, the operator, Swiss Post, and its vehicles (they had some interesting vans as well), with their always showroom condition soon became personal favourites. I now have quite a collection of models, books, many photographs and assorted items such as pin badges, centenary medal and driver's baseball cap.

Only when the later FBW C40ü type was seen did the unusual proportions register in my mind. Not only were the buses narrow, a sticker on the rear proclaimed them to be 2.3m wide, approximately 7ft 6in, with much wider rubber wheelarches, they had a very short front overhang, despite being underfloor-engined, and had a huge rear overhang. I now know that these handsome little buses had English Daimler gearboxes with Self-Changing Gears control, which sat well with the fact that they were right hand drive. This was always the case with traditional 'Alpenwagen' so that the driver was always on the edge of a precipice. The FBW C40ü entered service from 1956 and was almost immediately christened 'Haifisch' (Shark nose – well, Switzerland

A Schmoker Ramsieir & Jenzer-bodied Saurer at Interlaken West station in 1983, bearing the same BE 123516 registration plate as the vehicle photographed in 1977 and shown on the following page.

A Ramsieir & Jenzer bodied Saurer, registration BE 123516, of Gebrüder Schmoker of Beatenberg, near Interlaken, at Interlaken West station in 1977.

A Saurer of Autoverkehr Grindelwald between duties, hence the ropes, in its home town, again in 1977. The bodywork was also built by Saurer, identified by the prominent front dome.

is a land locked country and there wouldn't have been many people with first-hand experience of sharks!).

It became clear that there were in fact two separate types of bus operation with bus fleets devoted to each. There were traditionally two classes of bus, Alpenwagen, which was divided into five sets of specifications and Omnibus, which had seven. There was, of course, a separate touring coach fleet. The specifications laid down seating capacities, dimensions and other requirements, such as a minimum power to weight ratio (useful for mountain climbing!). These, together with protective import duties, ensured a guaranteed market for the Swiss manufacturers for many years. It also makes a nonsense of models such as a bonneted 1950s Mercedes-Benz, an American MCI coach or a Bedford VAL in Postal livery.

Traditionally, the drivers sounded their melodious three-note (C sharp, E and A in A major) post-horns, the tune from the andante of the overture to Rossini's

'William Tell'. This is sounded as the bus approaches tight bends on narrow mountain roads, many of which have access restricted to Post buses and residents. It is not widely known, however, that these horns also allowed post buses to 'talk' to post offices and to each other from a distance. Different combinations of the notes announce: 'departure of post', 'arrival of post', 'bus swerving out' and so on – so much more romantic (and probably more reliable) than radio or mobile phones.

Postauto, also called Poschi or Poschti in Swiss German dialect, is the standard term used in Switzerland for the motorized successor to stagecoaches. This linguistic anomaly also exists in the French and Italian-speaking parts of the country, where the terms Car postal (French) and Autopostale (Italian) are used. The current livery uses these as additional fleetnames.

The company

Postal bus routes are operated by PostBus, a division of the Swiss Post. Swiss PostBus Ltd became a separate subsidiary, based in Bern, in February 2005. The company operates 783 bus routes with 2,062 buses in Switzerland, transporting over 118 million passengers annually on its 10,429km-long network. The routes are operated by the Swiss Post itself or by local bus companies contracted to do so. Route networks are also operated in Lichtenstein and Dole, France.

PostBus has developed branded services in public transport, including:
* PostAuto: Bus services (urban, regional, long-distance, and sightseeing/holiday tours).
* PubliCar: Dial-a-bus service for routes with light traffic.
* ScolaCar: Small buses for student transport.
* VivaCar: Dial-a-bus service for disabled people.
* PostCar: Tourist travel.

The entire PostBus-owned fleet was re-registered during 2004, from P plates to Cantonal ones, so that there is now no clue as to the ownership of the bus. It has been a matter of interest identifying buses I see infrequently and attempting to match old and new plates.

Although the combination of mail and passenger transport had been a tradition for many years, the conveyance of parcels was progressively separated from passenger operation. This division became official with the 2005 conversion of Swiss PostBus into an independent subsidiary of the Swiss Post.

The contractors (known as Postautohalter) provide much additional interest. For instance, Gebrüder Schmoker of Beatenberg near Interlaken for many years operated small Ramsieir & Jenzer bodied Saurers between Interlaken and their home village in a pale yellow livery, until they were replaced in the late 1970s by the latest version in the new 'tricolour' livery – yellow and white with a band of red relief. They carried the same number plates as their predecessors, a fact made obvious by the same bends in the number plate which shows on a photograph. This operator, or its successor, for there is no trace of ownership on the buses, placed six Polish Solaris Urbino 12s in service in 2006, registered in a new series. Although these buses represent yet another a break with tradition they are worthy of their role, as when I first saw them they were already four years old and were in near perfect condition, inside and out, despite being used on busy town services.

A contractor which is well known for operating under its own identity is Autoverkehr Grindelwald (AVG), many of whose fleet carry Grindelwald Bus fleetnames on standard Post yellow. A number of Vetter Juniorbus vehicles are operated, some in full PostCar livery. AVG operate an amazing group of scenic routes radiating from Grindelwald. A particularly spectacular route starts from Meiringen, the town which gave its name to meringue, and begins an unrelenting climb through beautiful Alpine scenery on narrow private roads. A notable stop is Rosenlaui, where Conan Doyle had Sherlock Holmes stay during his pursuit of Moriarty, (Meiringen is so proud of its Conan Doyle links it has a Sherlock Holmes museum), then onwards and upwards to Scwarzwaldalp, where there is a ten-minute pause, arriving at Grosse Scheidegg an hour and ten minutes after leaving Meiringen. There is an 'interchange' at Grosse Scheidegg, where the bus from Meiringen meets its fellow from Grindelwald, which has climbed the other side of the mountain. There is a ten-minute wait for passengers to join from the hotel and then they return to their home towns. All this occurs at a bus stop outside a hotel on a plateau at an altitude of 1,961 metres, (over 6,000 feet), surrounded by the most spectacular mountain scenery and operates in a typically matter-of-fact and efficient Swiss manner.

The contractors often operated non-standard buses (or rather, more normal sized buses), on interurban services. I photographed a surprising choice in Schaffhausen in 1976, a Finnish SISU BT69, with Lahti body and AEC engine, in tricolour livery, operated by Rattin, a coach operator and provider of local urban

A PTT FBW C40ü 'Haifisch' again at Interlaken West station on a cloudy day in 1977.

A Finnish-built Lahti-bodied SISU BT69, with AEC engine, was one of several operated by Rattin of Schaffhausen in the mid 1970s.

services. Rattin's other services were operated by buses in a Swiss municipal like blue and silver livery; vehicles on these services included Saurer, Leyland Royal Tiger and Sisu.

The manufacturers

Most surprisingly, for such a small country, Switzerland had no less than six bus and lorry manufacturers, Arbenz, Orion, Martini, Saurer, Berna and FBW. It took a long time for FBW and Saurer to achieve their dominant positions in the Swiss bus market.

The history of FBW began in 1904, when the company founder Franz Brozincevic, a Croatian and a trained locksmith, opened a repair workshop for buses and trucks in Zürich. In 1911 'Motors-Franz' built the first 5-ton truck with shaft drive instead of the then-common chain drive on the European continent. In 1916 the acquisition of a bankrupt engine factory in Wetzikon led to the foundation of the Franz Brozincevic & Cie Wetzikon, leading to the adoption in 1918 of the FBW brand. From 1916 to 1985 the factory produced around 7,000 vehicles – trucks, tractors, army vehicles, fire engines, cars and trolleybuses, coaches and postal coaches. FBW was taken over by the Oerlikon Buehrle Group in 1978.

Adolph Saurer AG was an Arbon, Switzerland-based manufacturer of trucks and buses, under the Saurer and (after a merger in 1929) Berna brand names, and active between 1903 and 1982. Saurer ran subsidiary companies in Austria (1906-1959, in the end taken over by Steyr-Daimler-Puch), France (1910-1956, taken over by Unic), the United Kingdom (1927-1931, taken over by Armstrong Whitworth), and in Germany (1915-1918, taken over by MAN).

In Italy, Officine Meccaniche (OM) was for many years licensee of Saurer engines and other mechanical units, which they used in their own ranges of trucks and buses. From 1932 on, trolleybuses were a very significant segment of Saurer production. Typically Saurer, or Berna, trolleybuses featured Brown, Boveri & Cie or Société Anonyme des Ateliers de Sécheron (SAAS) electric equipment and Hess bodies. Saurer trolleybuses operated in many Central European countries.

In 1951 Saurer and its Italian licensee, OM, reached an agreement by which Saurer would market in Switzerland OM's light and medium-weight trucks and buses, using Saurer-OM and Berna-OM badges. This

Handbuilt 1/43rd scale Saurer Alpenwagen IIIa and FBW C40ü¸ 'Haifisch' by HB models, Czech Republic.

Some milestones in the history of PostBus

- **1849:** The creation of the postal stagecoach network.
- **1906:** First service of PostBus between Bern and Detligen.
- **1919:** Inauguration of the route crossing the Simplon Pass.
- **1921:** Grimsel Pass, Furka Pass, San Bernardino Pass and Oberalp Pass are open to traffic.
- **1923:** A three-tone horn is installed on the buses travelling on mountain routes.
- **1933:** The first PostBuses with passenger trailers commence operation.
- **1949:** The bus services of the Principality of Liechtenstein are operated by PostBus.
- **1959:** All buses adopt the now-famous yellow livery.
- **1961:** Last service of horse stagecoach on the Avers-Juf route.
- **2003:** For the first time, PostBus carried more than 100 million passengers.

was successful and lasted until the Saurer closure.

Declining sales saw the two leading Swiss truck makers, Saurer and FBW, forming a joint organization at the start of the 1980s called Nutzfahrzeuggesellschaft Arbon & Wetzikon, proceeding with bus and trolleybuses production under the NAW brand.

In 1982 Daimler-Benz had acquired a major shareholding in NAW and soon took full control; and in a short time dropped Saurer, Berna and FBW brands, while using NAW premises to assemble heavy haulage versions of Mercedes-Benz trucks. NAW went into liquidation in early 2003.

Old established coachbuilders Frech Hoch of Sissach, Vetter and Hess of Bellach had moved into semi-integral bus manufacture, the latter using Alusuisse technology and Scania chassis. Hess took over the rights to NAW trolleybus designs and has grown to the point of supplying export markets and producing the Swisstrolley range of 12m, articulated and double articulated LighTram, as well as a bus range which includes models for PostAuto.

The present day PostAuto fleet is, at first glance, made up of standard German imports, but that is only partly true. The city operations use Mercedes-Benz Citaros and MAN Lion's City 12m and articulateds, and now Solaris Urbino 12s, but interurban routes have very unusual Setras and Neoplans. Both types have the normal front associated with the bus, but straight sides and rear with two sets of plug doors give a special look.

Then there are Neoplan double deckers, 25 in all, but only three of them are the normal Skyliner type. The others are designated N4426/3, are coach-seated dual-door buses, with more upright styling than the Skyliners and the rear axles are set further apart, sufficient to be separated by bodywork. As there is little room for luggage, they often are to be seen towing trailers. One was exhibited at the UITP World Congress at Earl's Court, London in 2001.

The Swiss Post model collection

Whilst in Interlaken in August 1967 I bought my first PTT model bus. It was the first of many German Wiking models, a Mercedes-Benz O302 in yellow plastic with the PTT Swiss flag logo, what might be described as the 'line of least resistance' way of producing a Swiss Post bus model, with only a passing resemblance to the real thing. Several months later, I succumbed to the temptation and painted the roof cream, adding the red edged black band to make it as authentic as possible. I later regretted this, as it had ceased to be a 'perfect factory' example.

Is this the most spectacular bus stop in the world? A Grindelwald Bus Vetter from Meiringen awaits the connection from Grindelwald.

This Neoplan N4426 double-deck bus appeared at the 2001 UITP World Congress display at London's Earl's Court.

Years later, in August 1987, whilst on holiday again in Interlaken, I bought the last example in stock at Andre Luyton's model railway and gift shop for CHF10.50. You may think nothing of that, but it was an identical item from the same shop, and at the same price as the original 20 years previously!

As the operator placed ever more standard German built vehicles in service, so it became easier for the German plastic HO scale model manufacturers to produce convincing replicas of them.

From the same shop in 2004 I bought the first accurate large scale die-cast model of a Saurer. This was a 1/50th scale model of the RH 525.23 (Reise Heck – Touring coach with Rear engine, wheelbase and width in metric). This Saurer bus, the last bespoke one built for the Post by Saurer, was described in the 2006 Centenary book, 'Gelb Fahren', as the Rolls Royce of buses, and was to be seen throughout Switzerland until recently.

About three years ago I received as a birthday gift a magnificent 1/24th scale model, described on the box as Postauto P.2164 Alpenwagen Saurer 1951. Not only does every door and bonnet open, lights work, driveshaft turns, but also the seats are made in a very lifelike two tone leather look finish, and are soft to touch!

German-based Siku has recently adopted scales of 1/87th and 1/50th, at the same time as fitting more accurate wheels, which has coincided with a change of manufacture from Germany to China. A MAN Lion's City articulated bus in both scales and a 12m Lion's City in the latter are very attractive models on which the only obvious compromise is the appearance of the fleetname in all three languages on the same model and a bland 'CITY' destination. In reality the fleetnames would be in the one language of the area of operation.

A German-based model bus dealer insists that the PTT and PostAuto are second in worldwide popularity only to London Transport. They are with me, in fact, as my Swiss Post models are fast approaching a similar quantity to those of London.

My thanks to Isabelle Jampen, of Post Auto Schweiz, for her help in preparation of this article.

Representing a type of vehicle now very familiar on the streets of London, two Arriva ADL Enviro400s are seen at the Addington Street terminus, near County Hall, of the 341 to Angel Road Superstores, with a third identical bus lurking in the background.

Look in on London

RICHARD WALTER illustrates examples of London's current and recent bus operations.

Stagecoach also runs Enviro400s, one of which is seen approaching its terminal point in Whitehall on route 53 from Plumstead. This bus shows off well the 100% red required by Transport for London with no sign of the traditional Stagecoach stripes.

The first hybrid buses for London started arriving in late 2008 wearing a distinctive livery as shown on a Go-Ahead ADL Enviro400H operating through Victoria on route 24 to Hampstead Heath. More recent hybrid deliveries have had less prominent green branding.

Illustrating the now standard low-key hybrid branding, an Arriva Volvo B5LH with Wrightbus Gemini body crosses Waterloo Bridge heading north on route 76 to Tottenham Town Hall. There are now over 200 hybrids in London service.

The Abellio name has been on the streets of the capital since 2009, when it took over the Travel London business from National Express. An ADL Enviro200 Dart offloads passengers at Victoria Station before heading off to Canada Water on route C10.

Representing one of the early Scania/East Lancs OmniDekkas delivered to London operators is this 2005 Transdev bus on the 13 which runs from Golders Green to Aldwych. It is seen during the evening rush hour in Oxford Street with remnants of Christmas decorations still in evidence in January 2011.

More recently most London Scanias have been Polish-built models, as illustrated by this 2009 OmniCity N230UD of Transdev bound for Hounslow Bus Station in June 2011 on service 120 from Northolt.

Above: Towards the end of 2011, London mayor Boris Johnson fulfilled a manifesto pledge to remove all the 18m-long articulated buses introduced by his predecessor Ken Livingstone. Thus most of the capital's Mercedes-Benz Citaros met an untimely end, with only 12m rigid models now in service. An Arriva Citaro was pictured in Oxford Street in early 2011, a few weeks before service 73 was converted to double-deck operation.

Below: As the 100% red rule has been almost universally applied to buses within the central London area, the recognisable red with blue image of Metroline mainly survives on a few buses in the suburbs. A 2007 MAN 12.240 with MCV Evolution 26-seat body arrives at Hatton Cross on route 90.

In June 2011, one of Transport for London's newly-introduced Wrightbus-based hydrogen buses on route RV1 (which runs past many major landmarks, including Covent Garden, Tower Bridge and the South Bank) experienced a small electrical fire. They were temporarily replaced by diesel buses, including this First London Volvo B9TL Wrightbus Gemini body which is seen outside the Royal Festival Hall on route to Tower Gateway.

Above: There are remnants of what was once London Transport's Green Line network still running – but not always with green buses. A colourful Universitybus Scania K230UB OmniCity is seen in Victoria having arrived from St. Albans on the 712.

Below: Golden Tours added colour to London when it commenced open-top tour operation in June 2011. This is one of three Optare Visionaire bodied Volvo B9TLs which run the tour along with five semi-open-top former Stagecoach London Alexander-bodied Tridents. It was pictured at Hyde Park Corner before receiving its vinyls, with a few passengers trialling the tour.

A few independents also add occasional colour to the capital, including Ensignbus which runs both an operational and a heritage fleet in its striking blue and silver livery. A Volvo Olympian with Alexander Royale body is seen at Waterloo. The WLT 307 registration, originally carried by a Routemaster, disguises the origin of the bus, which started life in 1997 with Yorkshire Coastliner, at which point it carried a P-prefixed registration.

No selection of London photographs would be complete without a Routemaster, still to be found operating as a tourist attraction over sections of routes 9 and 15. The condition and appearance of the buses varies between operators with some wearing special liveries or adverts for London attractions. Looking smart in traditional London style is First's 48-year-old RM1735 at Hyde Park Corner in the summer of 2011.

Scotland
1979

There is something about a first holiday to Scotland, you want to see all the sights, the cities, the mountains and, in my case, all the attractive liveries carried by the buses. This was 1979 when standardised liveries were at their zenith in England and Wales, while in Scotland, even the standardised Scottish Bus Group fleetname style had yet to appear on all vehicles. It was still the days of taking summer holidays at the traditional time in August, not necessarily the driest time in Scotland as was soon to be experienced. A nine-day trip was planned which would cover most of the country although Aberdeen and the Ayrshire

DAVID COLE looks back to his first — and rather wet — Scottish holiday

All photographs by the author.

coast were eventually omitted. Leaving the Midlands on a Thursday, the rain was met around Lancaster. By the Lake District it was torrential and the pattern for the holiday had been set!

The first night in Scotland was spent in **Lockerbie** where a late arrival meant a long search for suitable bed and breakfast accommodation. The following morning dawned grey but dry and the opportunity was taken after breakfast to walk into the town centre. Here there were three buses awaiting departure, an anonymous blue Bedford SB bus and two Western SMT Leyland Leopards with Alexander Y-type bodies, one of each window layout. 1968 built DL2179 (KCS 150F) still carried the original Western script fleetname on its 49-seat dual purpose coachwork.

A few miles further north and the rain was back. A first stop was made in **Moffat**, famous for its toffee shop and little changed today. It is still a regular stop for coaches-but nowadays there is a purpose built coach park at the Woollen Mill a short walk from the town centre bus stance which is also occupied by a Galleon Tours coach. The Willowbrook-bodied Leyland Leopard bus was operating for Gibsons of

Lockerbie: Western SMT Leyland Leopard

Moffat on its long established service to Dumfries. 5208 HA was new to Midland Red in 1963, one of 100 Leyland Leopards that broke the pattern of 'home-made' single-deck deliveries. Sadly Gibsons ceased trading in 2008.

By **Edinburgh**, the rain had become incessant, so sightseeing was cut short in favour of heading for Stirling where bed and breakfast had been reserved for the weekend. Picking a convoluted route out of the city, a number of Lothian vehicles were seen laying over at the Granton terminus. With a transport department van behind, 1966 Leyland Atlantean 806 (EWS 806D) with Alexander bodywork appears to be attracting management attention. The rain finally eased by Stirling and a pleasant evening walk to the Wallace monument ensued.

The weekend in Stirling was mapped out to include the Saturday touring Fife and Tayside and Sunday in the Trossachs. Going east into Fife, the sun finally appeared and stayed through Kirkcaldy, St Andrews and across the Tay Bridge to **Dundee**. The blue Tayside Regional Council fleet was predominantly high-capacity double-deckers and no stretch of the imagination would have envisaged Dundee with a mainly single-deck fleet mirroring operations in Birmingham where I lived at the time. One of the older Tayside vehicles seen was

Above: **Moffat: Gibsons Leyland Leopard**

Below: **Edinburgh: Lothian Leyland Atlantean**

Dundee: Tayside Daimler Fleetline

Perth: Midland Ailsa

Callander: Eastern Seddon Pennine

Alexander-bodied Daimler Fleetline 302 (GYJ 402G) dating from 1969.

In the days before the Scottish Bus Group reorganisation which created the Strathtay business, Northern operated most services from Dundee bus station into the surrounding countryside and further afield. Setting off for the long inland journey north to Aberdeen, Alexander Northern Ford R1014 NT66 (WRS 666L) carries Alexander Y-type 45-seat bus bodywork, probably not the ideal specification for long distance travellers. Note the intermediate point information stuck to the windscreen, and the capacity load!

Heading back to Stirling through **Perth**, the sun had once again disappeared but the presence of several Ailsas on Perth city services brightened up the evening. Laying over before its next duty, Alexander Midland MRA1 (YMS 701R), a 1977 vehicle with Alexander bodywork, had already gained the latest Midland Scottish fleetname.

Fortunately, it remained dry for the Sunday tour of the Trossachs including the delights of Loch Katrine and later **Callander** where several Eastern Scottish vehicles were seen on tour work. ZS888 (GSX 888T) was a recently delivered Seddon Pennine 7 with underfloor Gardner engine and Alexander T-type dual purpose coachwork.

Monday morning, bidding farewell to Stirling until later in the week, the objective was Glencoe; however the rain was back and it was difficult to appreciate the beauty of the area. A night was planned in **Fort William** where accommodation was quickly found. The railway station had been recently relocated and a number of buses and coaches were parked up outside. Labelled for a Hebridean Tour, almost new Alexander Midland MPE347 (ULS 654T) catches the brighter skies of the evening as clouds still cover much of the Ben Nevis range. The Leyland Leopard features Duple Dominant 2 coachwork to bus grant specification.

Glenshiel had been recommended as a key scenic destination and fortunately, with brighter weather, did not disappoint. The day's final destination, **Inverness**, was reached late afternoon and accommodation for two nights secured. The city centre was considerably brightened by the Highland fleet in its poppy red, peacock blue and grey livery. The fleet had recently received its first influx of new double-deckers for many years, Leyland Fleetlines with ECW bodywork like D14 (SAS 856T) on route 2

Right: **Inverness: Leyland Fleetline**

Dundee: Northern Ford R1014

Fort William: Midland Leyland Leopard

Loch Ness: Highland AEC Reliance

crest. The former David MacBrayne coach is seen at the **Loch Ness** Monster visitor centre, the day's second destination after the battlefields of Culloden. Unfortunately, the only monsters seen were ceramic ones in the local shops.

All too soon, it was time to head south and this meant passing through **Perth** again. Here, one of the few independently-operated buses seen during the holiday was captured on film. Externally anonymous, UES 663K was a Willowbrook Expressway 002-bodied Ford R1014 operating for A&C McLennan of Spittalfield and is labelled for their service to Stanley.

Taking in some more of Fife before reaching Stirling for the night, there was time to solve the mystery of the Alexander Fife Leyland Nationals which had been seen on various SBG posters but noticeable by their absence in the first pass through the Kingdom. Reaching **Kirkcaldy**, I became aware that there was a town bus station as well as the sea front facilities seen previously, and it wasn't long

to Raigmore Hospital.

In contrast to its buses, the Highland coach fleet carried a blue and grey livery. This is seen to good effect on BA23 (PGB 708F), a 1968 AEC Reliance with Duple Commander coachwork which still carries the older Highland fleetname and eagle

Above: **Glasgow: Greater Glasgow Leyland Atlantean**

Left: **Perth: McLennan Ford R1014**

before the Nationals were found. FPN5 (HSC 105T) was an 11.3m model delivered in the previous twelve months.

Glasgow wasn't a planned destination, but no selection of Scottish liveries could be complete without the distinctive green, yellow and white Greater Glasgow PTE scheme. Accordingly, a quick break was taken from the motorway on the outskirts of the city where a regular procession of Alexander-bodied Leyland Atlanteans (and an Eastern Scottish

FS Lodekka) could be captured on one of the major arterial roads. LA846 (SGA 729N) on route 42 to Barlanark displays the panoramic window version of the Alexander body which would later exhibit structural weaknesses.

A final stop in Scotland was made in the sunshine in **Hamilton** where Central SMT produced numbers of Y-types, Leyland Nationals and Bristol FLFs. BE244 (CGM 744C) was a native Central SMT example of the latter with ECW bodywork and is seen leaving Hamilton for Glasgow. Perhaps fittingly, the last vehicle photographed before the long drive south to England was one of the FLFs involved in the exchange for Scotland's unloved Bristol VRTs between SBG and NBC. It would be eight years before my next trip north of the border, by which time post-deregulation competition was at its peak.

This is Bradford, where for a short time in the late 1990s First's buses were two-tone blue and carried Bradford fleetnames – barely visible below the cab window on the side of this Leyland Olympian with Roe body, one of 30 supplied to the West Yorkshire PTE in 1984.

Before Barbie

I like local liveries as much as the next person. You see a street scene with buses in Southampton in the 1970s, and you know it's Southampton because the buses are immediately identifiable. For Southampton substitute any other town and city you care to name. It would be going a bit far to say that, for example, the blue buses of bygone Bradford defined the city – but they did mean that when you arrived there you got some sense of local identity.

Of course, it's only enthusiasts who get excited by the colours of buses. When you're waiting at a bus stop and it's raining, you don't actually care what colour the bus is as long as it arrives before pneumonia sets in. And that holds true whether you're a proponent of local identities, or a supporter of corporatism. If you're waiting for a Stagecoach bus in Dover, it's of no matter that it's the same colour as the Stagecoach bus that someone else is waiting

Not all of the liveries obliterated by First's corporate 'Barbie' colours in 1998 were memorable examples of good design. STEWART J. BROWN illustrates a selection of First liveries, good and bad.

for at the same time in Dundee. Or in Drumnadrochit. All that matters is that it comes.

At the start of 2012 First announced a sort of localism agenda – bus devolution if you like – which will relax the dead hand of control from the Kremlin in Aberdeen. And it will also see local identities appear on buses. Good(ish) news for enthusiasts, although the local identities will be pretty low key.

All of which makes it appropriate to look back to the late 1990s before First went totally corporate. And what do you find? Depending on your viewpoint, a colourful medley of brightly-liveried buses ... or a disjointed hotchpotch of colour schemes which First did well to obliterate with its 'Barbie' liveries. And, I have to admit, when I look back at the pre-'Barbie' era, I tend only to remember the good, while conveniently forgetting the bad and the ugly.

So here's a selection. All of them united by the group's flying-F logo.

In Halifax First traded as Calderline, with the name again being underneath the cab window. The white-based livery was not one of the most attractive. The bus is a 1993 Volvo B10B with 51-seat Alexander Strider body. It had been new to Yorkshire Rider.

First used this bright livery in Leeds. This Leyland Olympian has the relatively uncommon lowheight Northern Counties body, easily identifiable by the shallower windscreens than were fitted to full-height buses.

Seen when new in the summer of 1997, this Mercedes-Benz in PMT's bright red and yellow livery gives prominence to the company's name. It is an O810D with 27-seat Plaxton Beaver 2 body.

Another bright livery was used by Provincial. This Leyland National was 20 years old when photographed in 1995, but looks smart and fresh. It features the flying-F logo, but otherwise no mention of First

Four Volvo Olympians with coach-seated Northern Counties bodies were purchased by Western National in 1993, at which point the company was part of the Badgerline group. Passengers wait in Plymouth to board a Torquay-bound bus in 1996.

Badgerline's green and yellow livery was distinctive, and was perpetuated by First. The Badgerline group favoured Dennis Lances with Plaxton Verde bodies between 1993 and 1996. This bus was new in 1993 and its original livery featured badgers on the side.

Bristol City Line was part of the Badgerline group and used a colourful livery, as demonstrated by a Leyland Lynx heading out of the centre of the city. Advertising on the side panels above and below the windows detract from the overall effect.

You can be forgiven if you don't remember First Skyblue, operating in Bristol. The Skyblue name is in corporate style, and the First name can be seen above the nearside front wheel. This is a Volvo B6 with Alexander Dash body which had been new in 1995 to Yorkshire Travel of Dewsbury. Skyblue was set up by Badgerline's Wessex subsidiary in 1993 to counter competition in Bristol.

Another blue fleet was the former Great Yarmouth Transport business, which briefly traded as Blue Bus under First ownership. A Wright-bodied Dennis Dart, new to London Buses in 1991, pulls out of Great Yarmouth bus station. It reached the coastal resort by way of First's ownership of CentreWest in London.

The Greater Manchester PTE and its Selnec predecessor set high design standards, including a distinctive orange and white livery. Then along came First, and after it purchased Greater Manchester Buses North, it took the orange livery to its ultimate, with just a thin line of blue relief. This is a 1996 Volvo B6BLE with 38-seat Wright Crusader body.

Above: **Before it was decreed that London buses had to be red, a number of the contractors providing services in the capital had colourful liveries, including First's London Buslines business, owner of this 1997 Dennis Dart SLF with Marshall body, seen outside Hounslow bus station when new. It carries route branding for the 403 which linked Richmond and Hatton Cross, but is seen on the 203 which, to confuse passengers, also ran to Hatton Cross.**

Below: **Prior to the formation of First, GRT had adopted a standard livery layout which respected the traditions of the operators GRT acquired. Here it is on an Alexander-bodied Metrobus in Leicester. Leicester City Transport's buses had traditionally been cream and maroon.**

Above: **The GRT layout, but using blue, was applied to Midland Bluebird buses in central Scotland. A Leyland Leopard with 53-seat Alexander Y-type body is seen in Edinburgh. Where the Leicester bus gives prominence to the First name, this one carries only the flying-F logo.**

Below: **Was this the worst of First? All over red, with no relief at all, was applied to the First Glasgow fleet. It is illustrated by a Volvo B10M with Duple 300 bus body in Hamilton bus station. The bus had previously been operated by Golden Eagle of Salsburgh.**